Y0-CPD-372

Julie Hudson, CFA
UBS Investment Bank

The Social Responsibility of the Investment Profession

Disclaimer | *This monograph draws on material from Julie Hudson and UBS Investment Bank. The views and opinions expressed in this monograph are those of the author and are not necessarily those of UBS. UBS accepts no liability over the content of the monograph. It is published solely for informational purposes and is not to be construed as a solicitation or an offer to buy or sell any securities or related financial instruments.*

RESEARCH FOUNDATION
OF CFA INSTITUTE

Statement of Purpose

The Research Foundation of CFA Institute is a not-for-profit organization established to promote the development and dissemination of relevant research for investment practitioners worldwide.

Neither the Research Foundation, CFA Institute, nor the publication's editorial staff is responsible for facts and opinions presented in this publication. This publication reflects the views of the author and does not represent the official views of the Research Foundation or CFA Institute.

The Research Foundation of CFA Institute and the Research Foundation logo are trademarks owned by The Research Foundation of CFA Institute. CFA®, Chartered Financial Analyst®, AIMR-PPS®, and GIPS® are just a few of the trademarks owned by CFA Institute. To view a list of CFA Institute trademarks and a Guide for the Use of CFA Institute Marks, please visit our website at www.cfainstitute.org.

© 2006 The Research Foundation of CFA Institute

All rights reserved. No part of this publication may be reproduced, stored in a retrieval system, or transmitted, in any form or by any means, electronic, mechanical, photocopying, recording, or otherwise, without the prior written permission of the copyright holder.

This publication is designed to provide accurate and authoritative information in regard to the subject matter covered. It is sold with the understanding that the publisher is not engaged in rendering legal, accounting, or other professional service. If legal advice or other expert assistance is required, the services of a competent professional should be sought.

ISBN 978-0-943205-75-5

21 July 2006

Editorial Staff

Maryann Dupes
Book Editor

Christine E. Kemper
Assistant Editor

Kara H. Morris
Production Manager

Lois Carrier
Production Specialist

The Social Responsibility of the Investment Profession

Recent Publications from the Research Foundation of CFA Institute

Trends in Quantitative Finance (April 2006)

Frank J. Fabozzi, CFA, Sergio M. Focardi, and Petter N. Kolm

> This introduction to recent developments in modeling equity returns provides a plain-English, formula-free review of quantitative methods—in particular, the trade-offs that must be made among model complexity, risk, and performance. The monograph also includes the results of a 2005 survey of the modeling practiced at 21 large asset management firms.

Investment Management for Taxable Private Investors (January 2006)

Jarrod Wilcox, CFA, Jeffrey E. Horvitz, and Dan diBartolomeo

> Private investors are more diverse than institutional investors and subject to complex tax laws. This monograph provides vital information—with a minimum of mathematics—on customizing applications of investment theory for a "market of one." Among the topics covered are the benefits of viewing private portfolio management as a manufacturing process.

The Dynamics of the Hedge Fund Industry (August 2005)

Andrew W. Lo

> One of the main reasons for the high interest in hedge funds is their performance characteristics: Many hedge funds have yielded double-digit returns for their investors and, in some cases, in a fashion that seems uncorrelated with general market swings and with relatively low volatility. Several recent empirical studies, however, have challenged these characterizations of hedge fund returns, arguing that the standard methods of assessing their risks and rewards may be misleading. This monograph reviews the empirical facts surrounding hedge fund investments and proposes several new quantitative models for modeling hedge fund returns, risk exposures, and associated performance statistics.

Tax-Advantaged Savings Accounts and Tax-Efficient Wealth Accumulation (June 2005)

Stephen M. Horan, CFA

> Until recently, the issue of tax-efficient investing has been largely overlooked by the mainstream literature. And simple heuristics to guide investors and their advisors are not always as obvious as they might initially seem. This monograph explores central issues surrounding the use of tax-deferred investment accounts as a means of accumulating wealth and presents a useful framework, grounded in basic time-value-of-money concepts, that can be readily implemented by investment professionals (U.S. as well as non-U.S. based) in various tax environments (current as well as those resulting from changes in the tax code).

Corporate Governance and Value Creation (May 2005)

Jean-Paul Page, CFA

> At its core, the goal of a company is to create value. And corporate governance should work to ensure that this value is created. This monograph describes what a value-creating corporate governance system should be like, establishes the standards that allow financial analysts to study a governance system, and suggests how analysts can analyze a company's corporate governance system.

Research Foundation
Literature Reviews

The Research Foundation is sponsoring a series of literature reviews on specific topics of interest to investment professionals. These reviews include an overview of the available literature and a description of the existing state of knowledge and major themes and subthemes associated with the topic. A thoughtfully annotated bibliography lists notable works. These literature reviews can be found at www.cfapubs.org.

Currently Available
Emerging Markets (May 2006)

Upcoming
Credit Derivatives
Private Wealth Management
Equity Risk Premium

Biography

Julie Hudson, CFA, is a managing director and heads the socially responsible investment team in equity research for UBS Investment Bank. In her 12 years at UBS, she has fulfilled a number of roles, including head of the customized research team, senior member of the global sector strategy team, and Asian funds research analyst. Her 20 years of market experience encompass global sectors, Japan, Asia, equities, and equity derivatives. She holds a BA from Oxford University, an MBA from City University Business School (now CASS), an MSc in financial economics from London University, and, most recently, an MSc in economic regulation and competition from City University.

Contents

PROFESSIONAL
DEVELOPMENT
QUALIFIED ACTIVITY

This publication qualifies for 5 PD credits under the guidelines
of the CFA Institute Professional Development Program.

Foreword

Many investors are concerned about the moral implications of their portfolio decisions as well as the investment returns resulting from these decisions. These moral implications include social, environmental, and religious matters. Some investors try to satisfy these concerns simply by avoiding undesirable investments. But no two investors agree precisely on what investments or social outcomes are undesirable or on how much diversification and opportunity the investor or investment manager should sacrifice in seeking to keep the portfolio "clean." In addition, some investors seek to use the investment process to further their social or other goals through proactive investment in companies or projects believed to do good, not just shunning those believed to create harm.

The kernel of the social investment movement can be traced back to the externalities theory of Ronald Coase, as he described it in October 1960 in "The Problem of Social Cost," published in the *Journal of Law and Economics*. This work transformed ideas as old as those of Alfred Marshall into an integrated theory of the influence of private market actions on other people who are not a voluntary party to the transaction.

The most obvious example is air pollution. A factory that produces a good in response to market demand for that good may also pollute the air, harming others who have not agreed to be harmed and who have not been compensated for the damage. The true source of this market failure, or inefficiency, is the incomplete definition of private property rights; if someone owned the air, he or she would charge the factory for the right to pollute it or prevent the pollution entirely.

Complete markets in resources such as air, water, the beauty of the environment, the health of the population, and so forth are not technologically possible. Taxation and government regulation are the usual proposed remedy, although "carbon credits" and other creative governmental attempts to impose an artificial market discipline on pollution are gaining acceptance.

Positive externalities may also exist. A real estate developer who builds an attractive building near my property may enhance the value of my property without my doing anything. All of these effects need to be considered when assessing the social costs and benefits of an economic activity.

The existence of externalities has given rise to discussion of "stakeholders," a word that may have arisen in contrast to "stockholders," the direct owners of a firm. Stakeholders—those who are affected by a firm's activities—are often said to include employees, customers, suppliers, the firm's community or neighborhood, and the natural environment.

                    ©2006, The Research Foundation of CFA Institute

Social investing attempts to influence outcomes more directly than can be accomplished with the broad instruments of regulation and taxation, or in ways that do not lend themselves to political action. Investors may, for example, wish to reward or punish a particular company for its behavior or may seek to affect a company's or industry's product mix, labor practices, supply procurement practices, or advertising.

The number of ways in which private market activity can affect public welfare is practically endless. I have provided a few examples that are easy to explain, but they are not necessarily the issues of greatest current concern to investors. Julie Hudson's monograph provides a rich treatment, covering many different types of social issues raised by portfolio investment.

Because social investment mandates have recently increased greatly in popularity—especially in Europe but also in the United States and other countries— a thorough review of social investment practices and issues is highly valuable. In *The Social Responsibility of the Investment Profession,* Hudson provides the kind of detail that makes it possible for investment managers and their clients not only to learn about the basic principles of social investing but also to put these principles into practice in a complex, multinational environment with varying customs and decision-making processes as well as diverse political, legal, regulatory, and accounting and disclosure requirements.

Hudson begins by describing the market for socially conscious investing around the world. She then proceeds to indicate how social investing interacts with the basic activities of financial management—the economic basis of decision making, the legal and regulatory environment, accounting and disclosure, and various competing theories of corporate governance. Hudson's third major section describes the roles of the main stakeholders in social investing. Fourth, she engages in a detailed review of disclosure and reporting issues. The final major section of her monograph discusses the ways social investing interacts with economic theory, including concepts from finance as well as welfare economics.

The Research Foundation of CFA Institute is especially pleased to present this extensive and richly detailed work.

Laurence B. Siegel
Research Director
The Research Foundation of CFA Institute

Preface

The field of social responsibility can be framed as the management of potential conflicts of interest between different societal groups, or stakeholders, with respect to economic, environmental, social, and ethical issues.[1] For the firm, corporate social responsibility is about its relationship with relevant stakeholders. For the investor, socially responsible investment (SRI) is about investing (either directly or through a relevant fiduciary) so as to take into account any exposure to the aforementioned conflicts of interest and their consequences. No less importantly, for corporations, managing the balance of priorities between stakeholders successfully may lead to an overall enhancement in performance in a broader sense, including financial. Therefore, the practice of socially responsible investment is also about identifying investment opportunities that deliver the best return within any relevant constraints.

At the level of the portfolio, at the risk of oversimplifying, this monograph identifies four approaches to SRI—exclusion screening, "best-in-class" security selection, engagement, and advocacy/activism. The analysis in this monograph suggests that the approach that works best (from the perspective of the investor, economics, society, and the environment) tends to rest on the prevailing corporate governance regime and on the perceived role played in society by markets in general at the level of individual countries. Furthermore, a rationale for each of these approaches can be identified within either economics or financial economics.

At the level of the firm, the extent to which corporate social responsibility is managed as an integral part of corporate strategy likely comes down to the corporate governance environment of the individual firm as well as the local country culture. The competitive playing field faced by the firm is also likely to have a strong influence on the extent to which the firm externalizes costs in order to compete or competes in order to internalize costs with a view to attaining superior overall performance.

In general, it could be said that, in any market system, it is the social responsibility of the financial sector to link social issues to finance where it is reasonable and feasible to do so and, of course, within a reasonable framework of accountability. The reasonable framework of accountability means it is also important to recognize when it is neither feasible nor reasonable to connect finance to social issues (or social issues to finance), which is, essentially, when ethics or value systems must prevail.

---

[1]This concept was also explored in Hudson (2005).

   ©2006, The Research Foundation of CFA Institute

Acknowledgments

I wish to express my appreciation to the Research Foundation of CFA Institute, as well as UBS, for supporting this project. In particular, I would like to thank James Sefton, Paul Donovan, Brian Singer, CFA, Richard West, and Stephen Cooper, all of UBS, for their helpful comments and suggestions. In addition, thanks must go to the writers of material referenced in this document, who without exception responded quickly to requests for permission to cite their materials and in several cases also made interesting and useful comments. Last but not least, I would like to thank Michael Oertli (Head of European Equity Research at UBS) and Erika Karp (Head of Global Sector Research at UBS) for their support. All errors, however, are mine.

Professional Development

Strengthening the Profession. Enhancing your career.

CFA Institute is your connection to the latest developments in investment management.

A Topic for Every Investment Professional

You'll find offerings in the following categories:

- Equity
- Fixed-Income
- Private Wealth
- Hedge Funds
- Firm Management
- Standards, Ethics, and Regulation

A Program for Every Learning Style

How you want to learn is up to you. You can choose to attend a conference, view a webcast from your computer, or read a print copy or online version of a CFA Institute publication.

Visit **www.cfainstitute.org/memresources/pdprogram/** to browse current and archived content arranged by topic, and to register for, subscribe to, or purchase educational offerings.

1. Definitions: The Global SRI Market

Socially responsible investment (SRI) is an approach to investing driven by the value system of the key investment decision maker. This decision maker may be a direct shareholder or a fiduciary acting on behalf of a third party who reflects the investor's return requirements, risk appetite, and investment constraints appropriately in the context of a portfolio. More specifically, SRI entails taking environmental, social, ethical, and governance factors into account in the construction of portfolios or in the choice of investments more generally.

This chapter takes a global perspective on the SRI market, reviewing definitions and exploring the implications of four widely used SRI portfolio approaches—exclusion screening, "best in class," engagement, and activism (see **Exhibit 1.1** for definitions)—for what they imply about financial market beliefs in the surrounding context. Key questions identified in this work are: What theories of finance shape SRI investment practices, and to what extent are markets viewed by SRI practitioners and investors as an effective medium of exchange for economic, environmental, and social assets and liabilities? Cross-border differences in SRI are superficially explored, followed by a look at the investor coalitions, rating agencies, and benchmarks specific to the SRI industry. The way SRI is practiced at the country level may depend, at least to some extent, on contextual factors, such as politics, legal systems, culture, the relative importance of markets versus the government sector, and the prevailing practices in financial markets in general because they influence the relationship between firms, investors, and society. The way SRI is practiced may, however, also say something about how well (or badly) market mechanisms are functioning.

The field of SRI has some common themes, such as the goal of treating stakeholders fairly. For example, the Calvert Group, in its Global Proxy Voting Guidelines for Calvert Family of Funds, states: "Well-governed companies are those whose operations are financially, socially and environmentally sustainable. Sustainability requires fair treatment of shareholders and other stakeholders in order to position the company for continued viability and growth over time."[2] Nevertheless, the importance of the values to SRI makes it inevitable that some SRI approaches are quite different from others, to the extent that some investments labeled "socially responsible" are regarded as the reverse by other SRI practitioners

---

[2]Found online at www.calvertgroup.com/pdf/proxy_voting_guidelines_new.pdf

Exhibit 1.1. SRI Definitions: Summary of Portfolio Approaches

Negative screening or "exclusion" entails the full avoidance of specific industries or companies on the basis of qualitative criteria. The usual exclusions include sectors in which the products are perceived to do harm if used as intended, such as defense and tobacco.

Best-in-class approaches involve taking a peer group of companies, usually the competing firms in a sector or an industry, and ranking them in terms of their environmental, social, governance, and ethical performance as well as their financial performance. The investment universe is constrained on the basis of the company rankings within the sector, and how tight the constraint is (top 10 percent, top quartile, top third, and so on) depends on the asset manager's investment philosophy.

Engagement takes the form of a constructive dialog between company management and shareholders. Engagement is consistent with an investment framework within which the shareholder acts like an owner, monitoring the company closely.

Advocacy/activism can be described as organized support of a specific cause. It is not necessarily the same as engagement because this approach involves acting as a group. Some may see activism as a first step, and others may see it as the next step if engagement (defined as a two-way dialog between shareholder and firm) does not have the desired effect. In practice, there may be some overlap between these two approaches.[a]

[a]Advocacy is the action of advocating or supporting a cause, according to Wikipedia, which also says: "Advocacy is an umbrella term for organized activism related to a particular set of issues. Advocacy is expected to be non-deceptive and in good faith." Advocacy is clearly a broad term that could be used to denote engagement, as defined above, or activism.

---

or investors.[3] For instance, some may believe the use of nuclear power to be a reasonable approach to the problem of global warming because of its low CO_2 footprint, and others may see the economic costs and environmental risks associated with nuclear power as simply too great no matter what the CO_2 related benefits. Each belief results in a very different response to the question of investing in nuclear power. Some portfolios exclude specific industries, and others have no specific industry exclusions but, rather, select investments in firms that do the best job of handling social issues raised by economic activity. SRI specialist benchmarks are similarly diverse in nature, and indices also vary. For example, the FTSE4Good Index Series excludes some industries, and the Dow Jones Sustainability Composite Indexes currently have no exclusions.[4] (See also Exhibit 1.4.)

The specific issues triggering the growth in SRI vary somewhat and with the passage of time. Broadly speaking, however, there appear to be four drivers of the SRI sector in most jurisdictions—faith-based or other ethical beliefs; social movements, often driven by political beliefs or by a reaction against political regimes; specific catalyst events that elicit a strong societal reaction, such as wars, famine,

---

[3]For an overview of this issue, see Statman (2005a).

[4]See Statman (2005b) for a review of the main characteristics of the Domini 400 Social Index (DS 400 Index), the Calvert Social Index, the Citizens Index, and the U.S. portion of the Dow Jones Sustainability Indexes.

©2006, The Research Foundation of CFA Institute

disease, or accidents; and last but not least, the values driving corporations (i.e., when they are perceived not to be aligned with the values of one or more of their key stakeholders).[5]

Currently, the drivers of growth and development in SRI continue to include ethics, social movements, event-driven catalysts, and corporate governance concerns. Issues that frequently appear in investment practitioner and other policy materials include diversity in the workplace, human rights, equity in the supply chain (fair trade), political risk, product safety, climate change, diseases in developing countries, and of course, corporate governance. For example, the issues that the ICCR (Interfaith Center on Corporate Responsibility) is currently focusing on include access to health care, human rights and other labor issues relating to the contract supplier system, corporate governance, access to capital, environmental justice, global warming, militarism and violence in society, and water and food safety and security of supply. The SRI proxy advisory services listed by ISS (Institutional Shareholder Services) are equal employment opportunities, greater diversity on corporate boards, abuses in executive pay, standards of environmental protection, the mitigation of climate change risk, the curtailment of abusive labor practices at home and abroad, and the improvement of consumer health and safety records. Alongside these issues continue to be the negative screening of portfolios in the traditional values-driven areas, such as tobacco, alcohol, specific political regimes, and nuclear materials.

In one sense, the SRI segment is global. The survey of research and other writings undertaken in this monograph suggests that SRI "themes," such as environmental stewardship and human rights, are reasonably universal concerns among SRI specialists. The main definitions of SRI—portfolio approaches such as exclusion, best-in-class investment, engagement, advocacy, and also, of course, community investment—are encountered in most jurisdictions. Although SRI can be described as global, it is also "local." The specific mix of portfolio approaches and the relative importance of other forms of social investment, such as community involvement and philanthropy, vary considerably by geography. In some jurisdictions, SRI portfolio investment consists primarily of exclusion screening. In some markets, best-in-class approaches predominate, sometimes in conjunction with engagement. In others, shareholder activism prevails. In yet others, environmental and social issues are more the preserve of government than markets and the SRI segment is almost nonexistent.

---

[5]For more information, see the fall 2005 issue of the *Journal of Investing*, which is dedicated to SRI, as well as the following websites (listed in Appendix B): Social Investment Forum (broken out by United States, United Kingdom, and Europe) and Ethical Investment Research Services (for the United Kingdom).

SRI Approaches and Financial Market Beliefs

The evolution of the SRI market in specific locations likely reflects prevailing (and highly contextual) beliefs about social issues. Furthermore, the role perceived to be played by financial markets, particularly with respect to the way in which they interact with other institutions in the broader social context, likely varies by country, which, in turn, is likely to affect the way the SRI segment is structured and the beliefs that underpin SRI activity. The next few paragraphs, therefore, consider what market beliefs might underpin the common SRI portfolio approaches.

Exclusion and Screening. Excluding segments of the market or individual companies on the basis of social criteria while being willing to accept the cost of a lower expected return to risk can be seen as consistent with the set of beliefs listed in **Exhibit 1.2** under the "Exclusion" heading. Exclusion screening suggests that investors, as a fragmented group, believe they have little power, at least in the short run, to influence individual corporations or financial markets. If Adam Smith's "invisible hand" dealt successfully with socioeconomic issues, such as the allocation of resources and the costs and benefits attached to them within society, the fragmentation of the group would be no problem. Exclusion of sectors or firms may at times suggest that, in the view of those following this strategy, markets are not succeeding in their role as intermediary between society and firm by allowing externalities to persist (note that Chapter 6 considers the possibility of a free-rider problem in the context of exclusion). For the ethical investor, the point is to perform within constraints. The exclusion investor might, therefore, validly regard any short-term difference between the portfolio and the benchmark in performance terms to be irrelevant. Furthermore, if the price of exclusion strategies is to accept lower risk-adjusted returns, then the exclusion investor is unlikely to believe that active fund managers have security selection skills sufficient to offset the loss of the diversification benefit.

The relevance of exclusion strategies for markets in general is that exclusion by large numbers of investors in a high-profile fashion can amount to a form of activism, and if this happens, it can have direct effects on companies and their cost of capital through markets (see Chapter 5 for more information). More generally, it may be said that trends in exclusion investment carry relevant information about paradigm shifts in society, and these paradigm shifts quite often become relevant to financial markets. South African investment exclusion and tobacco exclusion are good cases in point in the sense that sweeping changes did indeed eventually take place in South Africa (which is no longer a common exclusion on the basis of substantial changes in the political regime) and major changes are under way in the tobacco industry.

　　　　　　　　　　　©2006, The Research Foundation of CFA Institute

Exhibit 1.2. Summary of Beliefs by Portfolio Type

Belief	Exclusion	Best in Class	Engagement	Advocacy/Activism
Investors can influence corporations through markets	No (unless exclusions by a cohort of investors carry signaling information)	Yes	Yes	Yes
Markets influence the wider social context	No (but the impact of exclusion depends on how implemented)	Yes	Yes	Yes
Shareholders can directly influence corporations	No	No (influence is indirect)	Yes	Yes
The "invisible hand" works effectively to achieve Pareto efficiency	No	No (not all the time, but market mechanisms can be leveraged to correct social issues)	Not all the time, but it may be possible to guide it.	Not all the time, but it may be possible to guide it.
The efficient market hypothesis (EMH) is valid	Not relevant. The issue is to maximize wealth within values-based constraints.	Weak form may be valid, but semi-strong form may not hold.	Weak form and semi-strong form may be, but strong form not.	Depends on the underlying portfolio. Strong form probably not if advocacy is held to be effective.
Portfolio managers have stock selection skills	No (but hybrid strategies can be used, requiring selection and screening skills)	Yes	Yes	Yes
Market benchmarks reasonably reflect market risk	No. Exclusion strategies are necessary because markets may not always incorporate environmental and social issues.	Yes, to a reasonable extent, or it is believed that they will evolve to incorporate it.	Not relevant. With risk control through monitoring, the focus is on individual firms.	Yes, although probably over the medium to long term.

Best in Class. The very term "best in class" introduces the concept of competition into the SRI segment. Insofar as best-in-class investors set up environmental and social criteria as a basis on which firms may have to compete for capital in financial markets (as well as for success in their product markets), the possibility exists that they might influence the relationships between firms, markets, and society. In contrast to exclusion investors, best-in-class investors thus appear to be looking to leverage off market forces, implying a belief that markets can function effectively as an intermediary between the corporation and society. Best-in-class SRI portfolios are generally not benchmarked against SRI specialist indices but against conventional indices. This practice is consistent with a belief that active fund managers have significant security selection skills and also a belief that, imperfect though they may be, benchmarks constructed on the basis of the observed market portfolio are a reasonable representation of "the market" risk–return profile. Finally, the fact that best-in-class SRI asset managers aim to beat conventional market benchmarks by picking stocks on the basis of their environmental, social, and governance performance seems to imply a disbelief in the semi-strong form of the efficient market hypothesis (EMH). That is, they apparently believe that all publicly available information is not reflected in share prices, as represented by the benchmark (note that this notion is explored further in Chapter 6).

Engagement. The primary belief driving the engagement approach is that the shareholder can and should act like an owner and that firms will listen to shareholders who engage them on environmental and social issues. This approach rejects the idea that competitive markets in isolation are likely to constrain economic agents enough to ensure an equitable balance between stakeholders and, in effect, seeks to guide the "invisible hand" by influencing the behavior of firms (which, in turn, have a wider influence on markets in general and society). An engagement approach requires reasonably concentrated stock positions, needing less diversification within the portfolio; therefore, risk is likely to be viewed as absolute, rather than relative. The costs of lower diversification are expected to be offset on the basis that the interaction between shareholder and firm in the context of social, ethical, governance, and of course, financial issues should have a positive impact on the risk-adjusted performance of firms (see Chapter 5, which explores this issue). And this impact should also, therefore, have an effect in the same direction on portfolio performance. This approach, too, implies a disbelief in the strong form of the EMH.

Activism/Advocacy. Activism is often mentioned in the same breath as engagement, but it works differently because it can be confrontational, whereas engagement is more about a constructive two-way dialog. Activism may, however, be observed in action when the shareholder is constrained from acting like an owner.

If engagement (defined as acting like an owner) is not possible for some reason—for example, regulatory, legal, governance, or market frameworks can impede active ownership, and at times of financial distress, lenders may take precedence over owners—then the hypothetical asset manager seeking to follow this strategy has two choices: exclusion from the portfolio or activism. In practice, these apparently different approaches may end up having an equivalent effect if, as mentioned earlier, either is practiced in a vociferous manner by large investors or cohorts. Activism and exclusion suggest one belief in common—that markets may not be functioning well as an intermediary between firms and society.

Geographical Trends in SRI

Although in one sense SRI can be described as global, it is also "local," with quite different practices prevailing in different countries. The question posed here is why does the way SRI is practiced vary as much as it does by geography, particularly when many of the issues shaping SRI portfolios are global (see Chapter 2 for parallel paragraphs on corporate governance). The following paragraphs focus briefly on the United States, the United Kingdom, France, Germany, the Netherlands, and Japan and pick out some of the more significant differences in approach and seek to identify the reasons for them. Following that discussion, investor coalitions, rating agencies, and benchmarks are reviewed for what they may say about the relationship between markets, firms, investors, and society. Note that a question raised by these pages, but not addressed, is whether SRI funds have a home country bias and, if not, whether the investment approach that works optimally in the home base is applied to international portfolios.[6] In my view, it is likely that the exclusion and best-in-class approaches would be most relevant across borders (in increasingly global markets), whereas engagement approaches might need to be shaped to suit the local corporate governance approach.

United States. In the United States, the Social Investment Forum (2003) reported that more than three quarters of SRI funds under management were run on the basis of a screening or exclusion approach, with advocacy approaches accounting for most of the rest. The Social Investment Forum analysis does not distinguish between exclusion screening and positive and negative screening, so it is possible that some best-in-class funds are hidden somewhere in the total. Nevertheless, it seems reasonable to conclude from these numbers that the U.S. SRI market is primarily focused on exclusion screening, with best-in-class approaches on the basis of environmental and social performance accounting for relatively little SRI activity, at least compared with some European countries, such as the United Kingdom. The United States has a strong tradition of shareholder

---

[6]With thanks to Paul Donovan for raising this interesting question.

activism relating to corporate governance and social issues. Indeed, a notable feature of the U.S. SRI segment is the systematic gathering and publication of information on shareholder resolutions: The website of the ICCR (see Appendix B) is a good example. In addition, there are several corporate governance service providers, and the impact they may have cumulatively is to coordinate information. The question this description raises is why exclusion and activism are so prevalent in this SRI market? One possibility is that the SRI market has been shaped by the beliefs driving investment practices more generally.

The United States can be said to have been the birthplace of the efficient market hypothesis because that is where much of the groundbreaking research took place in the mid-20th century. Overall, a substantial number of market professionals likely believe the invisible hand to be highly effective and markets, in general, to be efficient. This belief may also apply more generally; for example, Martin (1993, Introduction, pp. 11–12) describes the dominance of the Chicago school of economics in U.S. policy circles. One can reasonably conclude that financial market regulation will also reflect such beliefs, constraining even those who might not believe fully in the EMH to invest in a way that is consistent with it, as Roe (1994) also suggests (see Chapter 2 for further detail). In short, diversification requirements embedded in regulation may have had the effect of impeding investors from "acting like owners" (owing to a fragmentation of share ownership). For example, Freshfields Bruckhaus Deringer (2005, p. 106) discussed the duty to diversify under ERISA law. An approach to SRI comprising mainly screening and advocacy with a strong element of activism (in short, a separation between SRI specialists and conventional asset management approaches) is indeed observed in the United States. Freshfields Bruckhaus Deringer (2005) referred to an ongoing debate as to whether the incorporation of environmental, social, and governance issues into investment decisions violates the modern prudent investor rule.

United Kingdom. In the United Kingdom, engagement is a significant activity for SRI specialists and the best-in-class approach is active. And both of these categories appear, anecdotally at least, to be growing more rapidly than pure exclusion. The United Kingdom has a well-developed financial market system and a well-established "equity market" culture, and market efficiency is part of the culture in the United Kingdom just as it is in the United States. Portfolios are also generally run on the basis of the efficient portfolio concept (see Chapter 6 for further discussion of the EMH in an SRI portfolio context), and the validity of benchmarks is widely accepted. But together with this, the corporate governance approach prevalent in the United Kingdom appears to place more emphasis than in, say, the United States on encouraging shareholders to exercise ownership (see pp. 29–31), and so the relationship between shareholders and company boards is relatively active in the United Kingdom. The corporate governance culture also incorporates elements of a stakeholder approach (see Chapter 2 for more detail), which may be one reason for the active SRI engagement market.

In addition, the regulatory environment in the United Kingdom is supportive of social responsibility. Starting in 2005, for example, it was expected that U.K. companies would be required to file an OFR (Operating and Financial Review), and although it now appears to have been scrapped, it is relevant for the philosophy it reflected.[7] The OFR was to cover all issues that were deemed by company management to be significant to the business of the firm, including environmental and social issues. The investment community awaits with interest to see whether firms, having put reporting mechanisms in place, continue to produce OFRs on a voluntary basis. Elsewhere, Freshfields Bruckhaus Deringer (2005) pointed to the goal of profit maximization as potentially precluding exclusion screening for U.K. pension funds but also gave a detailed definition of the concept of prudence in U.K. law, which includes taking *all relevant information into account* in making investment decisions (p. 86).

France. In France, where there is some negative screening—around 20 percent of policies according to Eurosif (2003)—best-in-class screening appears to be the dominant approach in the institutional investment segment, an unexpected discovery in a market having a blockholder or "insider" corporate governance culture (see Chapter 2 for more detail). Several points are noteworthy about the SRI market in France. Vigeo, a well-known SRI rating agency of French origin, may be unique compared with other rating agencies in having trade union connections at a high level in the organization. Nicole Notat, the founder and chairwoman, is a former director general of CFDT (Confédération française démocratique du travail), France's largest trade union. Elsewhere, according to a press release dated 24 October 2005, the French retirement reserve fund (FRR) is, as of November 2005, preparing its response to its call for submission to run funds under an SRI mandate, suggesting a relatively high level of acceptance of SRI as an investment approach in the institutional funds market. Two French houses (BNP Paribas Asset Management and AGF Asset Management) were founding members of the Enhanced Analytics Initiative (EAI), a group of asset managers lobbying for the "sell side" of the financial services industry to include extra-financial issues in research. Based on this analysis, the approach to SRI in France presents an interesting mix of exclusion, best in class, and activism [with, in addition, an active "solidarity funds" segment (Eurosif 2003)]. One goal of shareholders with an interest in environmental and social issues is identifiably to influence firms. In France, an important leverage point

---

[7]On 28 November 2005, the U.K. Treasury unexpectedly announced that the OFR would be scrapped. The speech by Chancellor Gordon Brown can be found online at www.hm-treasury.gov.uk/newsroom_and_speeches/press/2005/press_99_05.cfm.

for those shareholders with strong views on social or environmental issues seems to be the collective voice of financial institutions and other intermediaries. Recent regulatory changes appear to be supportive of this trend: Since May 2001, French firms have been required to publish social and environmental information in their annual reports.[8]

Germany. In Germany, the specialist SRI funds market does not appear to be very developed, being mainly the preserve of faith-based investment funds—these having a market share of just 0.4 percent in 2002, according to the Institut für Markt-Umwelt-Gesellschaft (IMUG). Freshfields Bruckhaus Deringer (2005) referred to the restrictive legal regime for mutual funds, in which environmental and social issues can be incorporated into investment decision making only if the fund contract so specifies. This situation may have its roots in the corporate governance regime (universal bank system) prevailing in Germany, which leaves only a minor role for the equity owner in relation to social issues. In addition, government-directed social or environmental investment is evident. Hence, in Germany, the alternative energy market is one of the fastest growing under the stimulus of government policy (see, for example, RWE's 2003 Corporate Responsibility Report, found at its website listed in Appendix B). Given the quite visible hand of government policy in Germany, it is perhaps unsurprising to find relatively little SRI activity in the investment funds market. But an awareness of the issues does exist. As in several other European countries, pension funds, according to IMUG, have been required (since 2002) to declare their SRI policy.

The Netherlands. In the Netherlands, where the minority shareholder has traditionally been relatively powerless (although this situation may be changing with the implementation of new corporate governance codes), almost all pension funds practice negative screening. According to Eurosif (2003), the Dutch tax office also has had some influence in shaping the SRI market by introducing the Green Savings and Investment Plan, focused on alternative energies (such as wind and solar) and such other activities as organic farming. These funds appear to have accounted for a substantial portion of the SRI market in 2002 (Eurosif 2003). Dutch trade unions also appear to have had some influence on the shape of SRI policies in the pension funds market. Because of the relatively limited role played by the minority shareholder in the Netherlands, it is unsurprising to find an SRI segment that is still developing. Several investment houses, however, are taking an increasingly proactive stance, which suggests that things may be changing.

Japan. In Japan, the minority shareholder has historically been relatively unimportant as a stakeholder. Thus, one would be surprised to find much of a tradition of SRI in the context of the equity market. As expected, Japan's SRI market

---

[8]See the EU website, listed in Appendix B, for more information.

appears to have a short history, coming to life with the establishment of the Good Bankers Company in 1998, with a further acceleration marked by the arrival of the FTSE4Good Index Series in 2004. The growth in assets under management and in research activity suggest that the relationship between firms and shareholders in Japan may be changing.

Summary. This cursory review of different SRI practices by country suggests that one may reasonably conclude that the importance of markets relative to other institutions (such as the government), the predominance (or otherwise) of efficiency-driven approaches to investment, the prevailing corporate governance regime and within it the relationship between firms and shareholders—all appear to play a part in shaping the SRI market. SRI is an investment approach driven by the values of the investor, but it is also a mechanism through which investors seek to influence markets, firms, and society.

Coalitions

Engagement and other strategies intended to influence firms entail a cost in terms of time and effort. Individual shareholders following engagement strategies may suffer a "free-rider problem" because they are sustaining research and other costs not sustained by everyone in the sector.[9] The formation of coalitions by investors having similar values and investment goals is a way of overcoming this problem. That is, by working as a group to change company behavior, appropriate costs, as well as any benefits accruing to the strategy, are shared. In the SRI and indeed the corporate governance field, many of these coalitions exist. Some of the better known are the SiRi Group, a coalition of 11 research and rating organizations; the Social Investment Forum (SIF) based in the United States, the United Kingdom (UK-SIF), Europe (Eurosif), and other locations; SIRAN (Social Investment Research Analyst Network), a social investment research network in the United States; ICCR, a coalition of 275 investors; and ECGS (European Corporate Governance Service), a coalition of several corporate governance organizations. Elsewhere, corporate governance and proxy advisory firms may lend some cohesion to activist activities simply by disseminating information.

Some coalitions are faith based. The ICCR, for instance, says on the home page of its website that it is an:

active international coalition of 275 institutional investors who use their religious investments and other resources to open doors at corporations and attempt to raise concerns at the highest level of corporate decision making.

---

[9]See Admati, Pfleiderer, and Zechner (1994, p. 1100) on the free-rider problem associated with shareholder monitoring.

The activities of this coalition include sponsoring shareholder resolutions, meeting with management, screening investments, and divesting stock together with a range of lobbying actions. Other SRI coalitions are networks of professional investors; some are confined to one country, and others are international. Some, like the SIFs, are a network of smaller country networks. Yet others are rooted in the work of nongovernment organizations, such as UNEP FI—a global partnership between UNEP and the financial sector involving more than 170 institutions whose goal it is to understand the effects of environmental and social considerations on financial performance. Some of these organizations work closely together. For example, according to its website, the GRI (Global Reporting Initiative):

> incorporates the active participation of representatives from business, accountancy, investment, environmental, human rights, research and labour organisations from around the world.... [GRI] is an official collaborating centre of the United Nations Environment Programme (UNEP) and works in cooperation with UN Secretary-General Kofi Annan's Global Compact.[10]

Some firms may share information more informally, too. For example, Hermes Equity Ownership Service states:

> In Europe, we exchange voting information with ABP, the Dutch pension fund. In North America, we work with California Public Employers Retirement System (CalPERS), and in Japan with Nissay Asset Management Corporation (NAM.CO), in exchanging information on voting in each region. These are local institutions which share our values and approach and which have supported us in our interventions.[11]

Coalitions may come into existence for many reasons. On the one hand, a group focused on front-burner social issues will likely gain wider attention than individual voices. On the other hand, coalitions answer the practical need for handling the huge flow of information facing anyone engaged in SRI research or investment. The most important impact, however, of investor coalitions in the field of SRI is their ability to attack the free-rider problem at a relatively low cost.

Rating Agencies

A number of rating agencies provide investors with company ratings in the areas of environmental, social, economic, governance, and ethical performance.[12] Although such agencies may operate in an independent and objective manner individually deriving company ratings, the very fact that the inputs to many of the rankings focus on similar social issues may mean that the rating agencies have a wider influence as a cohort. An additional, and important, point is that several of the rating agencies

---

[10] Found online at www.globalreporting.org/about/brief.asp.
[11] Found online at www.hermes.co.uk/.
[12] An overview of SRI service providers is given in Sparkes (2002, Chapter 11).

have also historically provided an engagement (or advocacy) service. On the basis of information in **Exhibit 1.3**, however, a trend appears to be under way for subscription rating services to separate from other services, such as research or engagement.

A striking feature of the rating agencies, shown in Exhibit 1.3, as a peer group is the frequent association between corporate governance (CG) and SRI. This association happens in two directions. In one direction, CG is the driver of SRI and a mechanism by which shareholders can influence firms with respect to specific SRI policies if their efforts are successful. Indeed, in some cases, the activity of SRI rating was only later added to the core corporate governance ratings (and sometimes to a preexisting engagement or advocacy) service. In the other direction, CG is subsidiary to the main SRI analysis. Some firms incorporate corporate governance into the CSR (corporate social responsibility) rating, indicating that whether CG is well or badly managed is in itself an SRI issue. Although the exclusion, best-in-class, engagement, and advocacy approaches are different, the association between CSR issues and the shareholder vote within several of the research agencies brings the strategies firmly into the same ballpark.

Finally, it remains to consider SRI benchmarks: The main features of a selection of indices are shown in **Exhibit 1.4**. These indices tend not to be used as performance benchmarks by SRI practitioners. But they are useful in throwing further light on SRI approaches in different jurisdictions. In the United States, the index providers are, without exception, research specialists rather than exchange-based index providers. In Europe, the index provider tends to be a specialist index provider working with an SRI research specialist (Dow Jones and SAM, FTSE and EIRIS). This pattern may be saying more about economies of scale and market structure in the index provider and SRI market segments than about the SRI segment per se. These geographical differences in the SRI index provider segment, however, appear consistent with earlier observations, suggesting a closer alignment between the investment generalist and SRI specialist in Europe/United Kingdom than in the United States. It is, however, also possible that this situation is changing. On 1 July 2005, KLD Research & Analytics launched the KLD Global Climate 100 Index, and in September of the same year, Dow Jones launched a Sustainability North America Index.

Direct Investment

In the SRI field, there are several forms of direct investment—a loose term that captures many different activities: community investment, sharing funds, solidarity funds, microfinance, venture capital, and other structures. In this monograph, the focus is mainly on portfolio investment. This focus was chosen not because philanthropy and community investment are unimportant but because direct investment is a broad, and quite complex, field in its own right, deserving of its own

Exhibit 1.3. SRI Rating Firms

Rating Firm	Scope	What Is Ranked
ISS	Originally U.S. based but now has global scope. Merged with Deminor (Europe, Belgian origins).[a]	Corporate governance (CG) ratings. No SRI ratings but proxy advisory and analysis in both CG and SRI. Deminor: corporate governance research and advocacy.[a]
GMI	U.S. origins; global scope.	Corporate governance research and rating service. A corporate social responsibility (CSR) rating, including environmental, health, and safety (EHS) issues plus regulatory and litigation records, is one of the inputs to the CG rating. Ratings are from a risk management perspective.
Innovest Strategic Value Advisors	North American origins; global scope.	Research, rating, and advisory on environmental, social, and strategic governance issues and their financial impacts. Global Compact assessment tool recently added.
Vigeo	Europe (French origins). Stakeholders include investors, trade unions, and corporations. On 15 June 2005, merged with Ethibel.[b]	CSR rating agency. Investor-solicited analysis on companies; company-solicited audit on CSR performance. CG is one of the inputs to analysis.
Core Ratings	Europe, Norwegian ownership. Subscription rating business sold to Innovest.[c]	CSR research and (formerly) subscription rating service. Inputs: governance and business ethics and environmental, societal, and employment issues. CG ratings.
IRRC (Investor Responsibility Research Center)	United States. Has historically provided corporate governance and SRI screening services (and no advocacy). Because of the acquisition by ISS (July 2005), IRRC's focus has changed.[d]	See left. IRRC is now focusing its attention on its macroview and thought leadership in the areas of SRI and corporate governance.
GES (Global Ethical Standard) Investment Services	Northern European origin; global cover of companies; globally networked through SiRi Group.	Screening for co-compliance with international conventions/guidelines on environmental, human rights, and business ethics issues. Ranking model, preparedness, performance in human rights, and environment. Engagement forum—member-based process for active ownership.[e]
EIRIS (Ethical Investment Research Services)	U.K. origins; global scope; nonprofit; five international research partners.	Research into and rating of the social, environmental, and ethical performance of companies. Environmental, social, and governance teams.

[a] See Deminor website.
[b] See Vigeo website.
[c] See Core Ratings website.
[d] See IRRC website; see also Sandeep Tucker, *Financial Times* (14 July 2005). Article archived on the website of ISS.
[e] See GES website.

Source: Rating firm websites as footnoted. See list of websites in Appendix B.

Exhibit 1.4. SRI Benchmarks

Index Provider	Index Name and Objectives	Construction Methodology
KLD Research & Analytics—provider of social investment research, indices, compliance, and consulting services to leading investment institutions worldwide	KLD's Domini 400 Social Index (DS 400 Index)—a benchmark for measuring the impact of social screening on financial performance.[a] Investment universe: United States. KLD provides several other indices. See website.	Exclusions of alcohol, firearms, tobacco, gambling, nuclear power, and military weapons. Evaluation of community, corporate governance, diversity, employee relations, environment, human rights, and product quality and safety issues.
Calvert—provider of investment products and services, including SRI funds and shareholder advocacy	Calvert Social Index—a benchmark for measuring the performance of large U.S.-based socially responsible companies.[b]	Excludes companies that produce firearms, tobacco, alcohol, pornography, casino games, or military weaponry. Stocks are included in the index on the basis of an evaluation of environmental, workplace, and community performance.
Dow Jones Indexes,[c] STOXX, and SAM. Dow Jones and STOXX are specialist index providers, and SAM is a provider of sustainability investment services	Dow Jones Sustainability Indexes are benchmarks designed to assist those who manage sustainability portfolios. Investment universe: global or regional.	No exclusions in the composite indices. Best in class in economic, environmental, and social performance (top 10–20 percent depending on geographical distribution). Subset indices provide the possibility to exclude certain industries.
FTSE working in association with EIRIS (note that separate to this, FTSE also has a corporate governance index in association with ISS)	FTSE4Good Index Series.[d] These indices are designed to measure the performance of companies that meet globally recognized corporate responsibility standards and to facilitate investment in those companies.	Inclusions: positive screening in environmental sustainability, relationships with stakeholders, and universal human rights. Exclusions: tobacco, weapons, and nuclear (power, arms, or processing). New criteria developed annually.

Note: This is not an exhaustive list of index providers. It is a selection of representative benchmarks (information correct as of December 2005). See index provider websites for other SRI indices.

[a] KLD website, indexes: Domini 400 Social Index.
[b] The website of Calvert: Calvert Social Index.
[c] See the website of Dow Jones Indexes.
[d] See the website of FTSE: FTSE4Good, Inclusion Criteria, and other reports on the website.

Source: Index provider websites as footnoted. See website list in Appendix B.

publication.[13] Straight philanthropy reflects a belief that those who have prospered should give something back. It takes several forms. In some jurisdictions, "sharing" funds are mandated to allocate a proportion of either investment fees or dividends to community projects.[14] In one sense, sharing funds or other structures that make a direct philanthropic contribution are similar to exclusion funds: They reflect the view that higher costs are acceptable if the aim is to do good. But exclusion funds are closer to the market than sharing funds and similar structures. Exclusion funds can be said to incorporate a long-term performance "option"—namely, the possibility that the view reflected in exclusion portfolios may, at some stage, become relevant to the broader market and hence that the market may act as a redistribution mechanism. Straight philanthropy, in effect, bypasses markets as an adequate means of wealth distribution and goes direct. How firms deal with community investment or other forms of philanthropy may, in the context of other information, say something about their general approach to governance and, therefore, may also be a relevant input to analysis at times.

Socially responsible investment is sometimes thought to be synonymous with community investing and other forms of philanthropy (and with negative screening). As the earlier discussion should have made clear, SRI is a rather more complex discipline. Perhaps the most important point to drop out of this chapter is that the definition of the SRI "market" in different jurisdictions, particularly with respect to the way it relates to corporate governance, may be explained not only by contextual factors (such as politics, legal systems, culture, the relative importance of markets versus the government sector, and the prevailing practices in financial markets in general) but also, to a large extent, by prevailing beliefs relating to the efficiency of economies and markets. Since the appearance of the first anomaly literature, together with the development of the field of behavioral finance (not to forget the growth of the hedge fund industry in recent years), efficiency-driven approaches have been increasingly open to challenge. The persistence of SRI as a discipline, its steadily increasing profile, and its close alignment with corporate governance can be seen as another window on this trend.

---

[13]See the Institute for Strategy and Competitiveness website under the heading Competition and Society for some material on philanthropy and CSR. The address for the website is given in Appendix B.
[14]Eurosif (2003, p. 64).

2. SRI's Relationship with Other Investment Disciplines

A financial market is a social organization fulfilling a specialist role, namely, the facilitation of exchange in financial assets and liabilities. It plays this role in a wider social context by indirectly influencing the exchange of many other social goods—labor, capital, and know-how to name just three. Social issues, therefore, almost inevitably run through all the investment disciplines that professional financial analysts and asset managers draw on to inform investment decisions. Some of those disciplines—such as economics, regulation, corporate governance, and accounting and disclosure—are about other social organizations or institutions (e.g., governments and corporations) that can also play a role in connecting finance to social issues or indeed social issues to finance. This chapter presents an overview of these areas with a view to considering how SRI, as defined in Chapter 1, fits into the broader investment picture.[15]

Economics

Socially responsible investment can be said to be about maximizing welfare (rather than wealth *tout court*). In this regard, it can be said to have a broader focus than financial economics but one that is nevertheless recognized by many economic disciplines.[16] "Welfare analysis concerns itself with the evaluation in the effects of changes in the consumer's environments on [his or her] well-being" (Mas-Colell, Whinston, and Green 1995, p. 80). Welfare economics is more commonly applied in emerging market contexts than developed market contexts (but also relevant to economic regulation in developed markets) and recognizes that markets are not always efficient and considers the consequences of market failure:

> An externality is present whenever the well-being of a consumer or the production possibilities of a firm are directly affected by the actions of another agent in the economy. (Mas-Colell, Whinston, and Green 1995, p. 352)

> Under a market system it is the relation between fixed cost and market size that determines which products are produced and which are not produced. A market system will not automatically produce all socially desirable products. (Martin 1993, p. 16)

---

[15]Note that this chapter contains an inevitable element of idea exploration, which means more questions may be raised than fully answered. The approach is emphatically empirical, based on the observation of practices in the market, and this may (with luck) raise some interesting questions.

[16]With thanks to James Sefton for helping to clarify some of the points made in this chapter.

When efficient conditions have not been reached in the context of any given market, the implication is that resources have not been successfully distributed, at a fair price, between the relevant stakeholders or market participants. In short, markets have not cleared at a competitive equilibrium. Firms or businesses that are perfectly efficient in the financial (or productive) sense may turn out to be inefficient when welfare effects are considered, which is what SRI is often about. Manufacturing while polluting the environment, underpaying the workforce, or outsourcing to developing markets for extremely cheap raw materials may seem to translate to maximum operating efficiency (and profit margins), but the operating efficiency may be possible only in the absence of a market or other mechanism that properly allocates relevant but unrecognized costs (and hence the related profit margins may be illusory and temporary).

Where the efficiency measures used by firms and other bodies are accounting profit and cash flow, there may be no means of incorporating environmental and social costs into these frameworks. Thus, conventional economic analysis and conventional accounting frameworks may mask economic inefficiency. This problem has been recognized in some quarters. Environmental economics, for instance, recognizes that GNP as traditionally calculated masks the depletion of natural resources and fails to incorporate the true costs of economic activity that pollutes the environment—hence the development of "green" national accounts.[17] In practice, green national accounts can be difficult to put into use. As Hamilton and Lutz (1996, p. 20) pointed out, in an economic context, estimating the cost of protecting the environment in the presence of production technologies that simultaneously increase production and reduce pollution is not easy.

The question is why such policies should matter to analysts and portfolio managers. Is not the job of an asset manager simply to manage a portfolio in such a way that it meets the required benchmark return within desired risk constraints? Several possible reasons can be identified for why such policies should matter to portfolio managers. First, investors do not all share the same utility; therefore, they do not necessarily look to maximize wealth if, for example, doing so entails placing less emphasis on caring about other people. Some investors look to maximize wealth subject to constraints, some of which may be risk based and some of which may be values based. Second (and related), a consideration of economic welfare may highlight situations in which firms are not operating within reasonable constraints as judged by some investors, with potential implications for fiduciary duty. Third, economic inefficiencies often involve an inefficient transfer of resources, and over time, this situation may reverse—whether because markets "correct" or because government bodies introduce rules and regulations to redress the balance—and

---

[17]For a full account of environmental and economic accounting for national accounts, see UN, EC, IMF, OECD, and World Bank (2003).

financial consequences may ensue. For analysts specializing in utility stocks or pharmaceutical stocks, such considerations are routine. Fourth, society may come to regard economic inefficiencies as unjust, and any activism ensuing from this belief could result in disruptive change to a firm's key markets.

The field of welfare economics, together with the associated disciplines of development economics and economic regulation, is first and foremost about social, environmental, and economic welfare rather than "wealth." Nevertheless, the distinction between economic welfare and economic wealth is not always clear-cut. Just as welfare economics and the associated disciplines of development economics and the economics of regulation deal with "nonmarket" effects of economic activity (environmental and social), so too does SRI deal with the environmental, social, and economic consequences of corporate activity.

Legal and Regulatory Environment

When markets are unable to resolve distribution issues optimally, regulation is often what fills the gap. Regulatory trends and changes may affect the expected cash flow stream of firms. Changes in the legal or regulatory regime are most obviously relevant to the SRI market because regulation is one means by which costs that have been externalized can be put back to the firm. But because the mechanisms described in this chapter are means by which society realigns incentives (both financial and nonfinancial) in such a way as to ensure a more balanced treatment of stakeholders, this area is inevitably also relevant to anyone involved in making investment decisions.

This monograph does not give sufficient scope for an exhaustive survey of regulatory change worldwide, but a summary with a few examples, given in **Exhibit 2.1**, should serve to illustrate this important point. For example, new markets can be created, as in the cap and trade schemes observed in several jurisdictions in the context of environmental issues; the financial impact of such schemes is widely recognized—for instance, the so-called SO_X (SO_2) and NO_X

Exhibit 2.1. Summary: Regulatory Approaches to Market Inefficiencies

Regulatory Approach	Effectiveness	Impact on Company Performance/Valuation	Example
Create new markets	Depends on the design and implementation of the new markets.	Different impacts on parts of the "food chain"; possible effects on margins and profitability, also valuation. Scope for transfers of wealth within the food chain.	Cap and trade schemes—emissions trading in Europe; SO_2 trading in the United States.

(continued)

Exhibit 2.1. Summary: Regulatory Approaches to Market Inefficiencies (continued)

Regulatory Approach	Effectiveness	Impact on Company Performance/Valuation	Example
Create insurance vehicles	Depends on the design and implementation of new or existing, and related, markets. Insurance markets are considered to be "incomplete," giving rise to moral hazard.	Transfer of risk between companies and industries means likely valuation impact should follow. Risk (volatility) should fall if risk becomes better dispersed.	Weather insurance. Catastrophic events insurance.
Financial or other nonmonetary rewards/ awards	Depends on how administered and on how widely accepted. Can introduce a "race to the top" effect if so.	May affect profits, therefore, also valuation. May affect relative competitiveness, valuation.	ENERGY STAR program, United States/Japan.
Subsidize new or nascent technology (e.g., through favorable tax treatment)	Depends on how administered. Subsidies can potentially act as a catalyst for market development or can distort markets.	Impact on profits (through increased costs) should translate to valuation impact. Competition effects also possible.	Biofuel market in the United States; alternative energy markets in Europe.
Taxes, fines, or other penalties	Depends on how effectively collection can be made. Relies on adequate infrastructure and lack of loopholes; opportunity for "regulatory arbitrage."	Impact on profits (through increased costs) should translate to valuation impact. Competition effects also possible.	Cleanup requirements, EPA. CERCLA, United States. Polluter pays regulation, Europe.
Legal action	May take a very long time; direction of impact likely to be along the right lines, scale may not be.	One-off impact on profits. Distribution of cost may be unfair, could have "competition" effects.	Punitive damages or other substantial financial penalty (e.g., from classaction lawsuits).
Disclosure/reporting— mandatory or voluntary	A cost to firms. Better transparency if well implemented.	Introduces potential for "race to the top" if investors take account of this information.	REACH (chemicals regulation Europe). Key performance indicators in CSR reports.
Outright prohibition in the law[a]	Depends on how well policed. May also depend on local culture.	If the law is obeyed, a level playing field is created for firms. If not, there may be a short-term cost advantage to some firms (at the cost of higher risk).	Narcotics, money laundering, arms trade.

[a]With thanks to Paul Donovan for suggesting this additional row.

Source: Based on Hudson (2005).

programs in the United States and the Emissions Trading Scheme (ETS) in Europe. Insurance vehicles can be created to spread risk or other costs across several stakeholders; in this case, new vehicles tend to be market led because the insurance sector responds to demand for new products to cover new risks. Insurance markets, however, are known to be "incomplete," so other mechanisms can sometimes be brought into play through regulation (e.g., regulatory reserves, such as those found in some pension fund markets). Sometimes financial or other nonmonetary rewards or awards can be applied to create "race to the top" competition. The Energy Star programs in the United States and Japan may be good examples. Sometimes, what is needed is a catalyst to start new practices. In such cases, subsidizing new or nascent technology in the early stages of development may be effective, for example, through favorable tax treatment or other concessions. This approach is appearing in some alternative energy markets in Europe and, indeed, the United States since the passing of the Domenici–Barton Energy Policy Act of 2005. Taxes, fines, or other penalties are often encountered in the context of environmental problems (such as clean-up requirements or the requirement to pay for natural resource damage). In some jurisdictions, the legal system gives scope for punitive damages.

As the previous paragraphs suggest, regulation varies from one country to the next, which can, in itself, have several effects. First, if regulation is directed by individual countries at a global problem, such as climate change caused by CO_2 emissions, the result may be less effective than if countries address the problem together and may also bring about shifts in comparative advantage between firms or sectors from one country to the next. Second, regulatory differences may be a source of risk in a very general sense as well as a source of risk specifically relevant to SRI. Examples include issues relating to human rights or resources within the supply chain, to fair trade in general, and of course, to country exclusions on the basis of certain political regimes, such as with South Africa historically. At times, firms state in financial reviews that they obey the law in all countries where they operate. In practice, doing so may imply inconsistent standards of social or environmental responsibility.

Last but not least, disclosure and other reporting requirements, which can be mandatory or voluntary, can be tremendously effective in bringing social issues "to market." Currently, for example, many firms have begun to report environmental and other CSR key performance indicators on a voluntary basis, giving analysts a new and potentially rich source of data for analysis. Elsewhere, European regulations for electronic waste and chemicals reporting, still under development, are likely to have considerable impact on electronics and chemicals firms as well as firms in their food chain.[18] Good quality disclosure (or the lack thereof) can have far-reaching impacts in many contexts. Without effective disclosure, most of the aforementioned regulatory mechanisms are unlikely to work.

Accounting and Disclosure

Good disclosure is critically important for financial markets: Without sufficient disclosure, markets would be unlikely to function properly. Much of the regulation on disclosure in financial markets revolves around making sure market players are on a level playing field with respect to access to information.

The "culture" of the accounting system in any given country is likely to have been shaped by some of the influences already identified in this monograph as shaping practices in SRI, such as the political and legal systems, the prevailing culture, and the structure of finance systems.[19] The accounting system is likely to have been most significantly influenced by the prevailing legal regime (whether common law or civil code) and the prevailing capital market structure (whether equity, bank, or insider dominated). At the risk of generalizing, one would expect principles-based accounting systems to be a feature of countries having a common law system (such as the United Kingdom) and rule-driven accounting systems to be a feature of civil-code-based countries. In a principles-based system, the onus is on firms reporting CSR issues to identify issues that are material (in an accounting sense) rather than simply to make reports and disclosures according to set rules (see Chapter 4 for more information). Principles-based reporting regimes leave scope for firms to *compete* (see also Chapter 1) on the quality of their disclosure. SRI implemented on the basis of engagement or best-in-class approaches would, all other things being equal, be expected to be more likely in the context of a principles-based accounting regime.

The relative importance of equity investor versus creditor may also have a bearing on the shape and implementation of accounting regulation from one region to the next as well, of course, as on the implementation of all investment, including SRI. If the creditor is more important, then reporting may tend to be more conservative—the main objective being to protect the interests of lenders. If society at large is regarded as the most important stakeholder, accounting frameworks may tend to reflect government policy (and would be expected to be shaped by the underlying goal of raising taxes). If equity investors are regarded as the main stakeholders, financial statements would be expected (obviously within the scope of "fair view"

---

[18]For electronic waste, see Directive 2002/96/EC, found online at http://europa.eu.int/eur-lex/pri/en/oj/dat/2003/l_037/l_03720030213en00240038.pdf, and for chemicals, see REACH (Registration, Evaluation and Authorization of Chemicals), found online at http://europa.eu.int/comm/environment/chemicals/reach.htm.

[19]See also Roberts, Weetman, and Gordon (1998).

requirements) to focus more on firm value. The several approaches to accounting for R&D (research and development) identifiable in global and country-level accounting standards tabulated in **Exhibit 2.2** are a good example: R&D is more likely to be viewed as a generator of value in equity-based capital market regimes and as a cost in credit or government (tax) dominated regimes. Under the influence of global accounting systems, approaches may be converging. Nevertheless, the contrast between Germany, on the one hand, and the United Kingdom and IAS, on the other hand, in Exhibit 2.2 is of note. France is somewhere between the two, allowing the recognition of research as an asset but over a limited time period.

Exhibit 2.2. R&D Accounting Summary

Country	R&D
International: International Accounting Standard (IAS) 38	Research should be expensed in the relevant accounting period. Development can be recognized as an asset.
France	Pure research expensed. Applied research can be recognized as an asset; amortization maximum five years.
Germany	Internally generated intangibles (including R&D) may not be recognized.
United Kingdom	SSAP13 requires all research to be expensed but development can be recognized as an asset subject to certain criteria.

Source: Table constructed from information given in Roberts, Weetman, and Gordon (1998).

Accounting frameworks are designed around economics and markets and alongside other contextual institutions and frameworks. The risk inherent in accounting frameworks developed in this manner is that they may be ill-equipped to recognize economic costs and benefits in the widest sense, and therefore, the risk is that they may prevail against the recognition of social and environmental issues as being relevant to markets.

The aim of the accruals approach to accounting is to present economically significant data. Accounting rules then apply constraints to make sure accruals are applied in a prudent fashion. International Accounting Standard (IAS) 18: *Revenue*, for example, states that revenue from the sale of goods should be recognized when "it is probable that future economic benefits will flow to the entity and these benefits can be measured reliably" (IASB 2004, p. 888). IAS 37: *Provisions, Contingent Liabilities and Contingent Assets* states that liabilities that are uncertain in terms of amount or timing should be recognized only when an entity "has a present obligation (legal or constructive) as a result of a past event; it is probable that an outflow of resources embodying economic benefits will be required to settle the obligation; a reliable estimate can be made of the obligation" (IASB 2004, p. 1529). Contingent liabilities can be disclosed (if they are not remote) but should not be recognized (see IASB 2004, p. 1532), which, of course, goes right back to points raised in the section on economics. Even if it is reasonably certain that costs have been passed from firm to society or vice versa, it is often the case that environmental, social, and ethical costs and benefits (or assets and liabilities) may not be certain to crystallize and cannot be measured. Therefore, they may not be disclosed.

The job of the financial analyst is to take account of value created or destroyed from whichever part of the business (financial, economic, environmental, social) by interpreting financial statements delivered under the relevant framework. Ultimately, putting a number on some aspects of value created or destroyed may be impossible, even if the information is disclosed (in textual commentary, for instance). In practice, regulatory frameworks are often required, as seen in the previous section, for this disclosure to take place. Even this regulation may not be sufficient all the time.

Attaching a price to environmental activity is (relatively) feasible. Thus, many of the examples given in Exhibit 2.1 come from that area. Other issues are not so straightforward. Policies designed to improve diversity in the workforce may entail an up-front cost, and the benefit may be neither certain nor measurable because it cannot be isolated from everything else. Hence, without outside pressure (such as peer group competition or regulation), firms have no incentive to redress the balance. For example, a provision of free HIV/AIDS treatment to the workforce will entail an up-front cost, and even if benefits are now reasonably predictable on the basis of experience (longer working lives of employees), the benefit (which is reasonably certain to accrue but unknown in terms of timing and difficult to value) cannot be reflected in financial statements.[20] It should be stressed that this is in no way a criticism of accounting frameworks in any country. The frameworks that have been developed over the years simply reflect what was required at the time. Above all, according to Roberts, Weetman, and Gordon (1998), the history of accounting indicates that accounting bodies respond to the requirements of their main stakeholders. Specific combinations of accounting frameworks and capital market structures are likely to reflect the priorities of the predominant stakeholder in context. This balance, then, is likely to determine (1) which are the most important "CSR" issues, (2) how the issues are handled, and (3) whether they have financial effects.

Little doubt exists that accounting conventions can and do influence the way in which CSR issues play out. A firm's financial statements often set the terms of

---

[20]See also F&C Asset Management and UBS (2005).

the contract between specific stakeholders and are at the same time affected by it—the most obvious example being management compensation—which raises a highly significant issue:

> Using accounting measures of performance to determine payments to managers gives managers a direct interest in the choice among different accounting techniques. . . . The evidence of Healey and Kaplan (1985) indicates that the firm's choice of accounting-accrual policy is influenced by the effect of those policies on bonuses to managers. Other studies . . . find that bonuses increase the probability of selecting corporate accounting procedures that shift accounting earnings from future periods to current periods. (Jensen 2003, p. 147)

Corporate Governance

In Chapter 1, the structure of the SRI funds market (which was found to be primarily focused on negative screening in some contexts and primarily about engagement and best-in-class portfolio selection in others) was attributed to context. The particularly critical aspect with respect to SRI practices in context is the prevailing relationship between the corporation, its management, and its owners. At this juncture, reviewing prevailing theories of corporate governance in the context of SRI is thus useful. The best known are the agency, stewardship, and stakeholder theories of corporate governance. As suggested in Chapter 1, the regional differences in the SRI segment observed in the previous section may have something to do with the prevailing corporate governance regime.

Agency Theory. Agency theory deals with the incentive problems that arise out of the separation of ownership and control:

> Private enterprise has been trying during the past fifty years to solve for itself the essential problem . . . namely, how to establish an efficient system of production in which management and responsibility are in different hands from those which provide the capital, run the risk, and reap the profit. (The Liberal Industrial Enquiry of 1926–1928 in Britain, as quoted in Cadbury 2002)

The main prediction of agency theory is that corporate managers will behave opportunistically to their own advantage. The issue, in an agency context, is thus to arrive at a sufficiently strong mix of controls, checks, and balances to align the incentives of company management with those of shareholders. A number of mechanisms are relevant to this effort. Competitive markets are widely believed to be an effective indirect controlling mechanism. Equity-linked compensation is an example of a mechanism that was introduced in several countries in the expectation that it might better align the incentives of management with those of shareholders. And transparent accounting systems should enhance the ability of shareholders to monitor the firm. Detailed regulatory requirements with respect to shareholder votes may, however, be required if acceptance of the agency problem is widespread.

That is, if shareholders feel disenfranchised, they may not bother to vote, exacerbating the separation between ownership and control even further. For example, in the United Kingdom in the 1990s, the government warned that if voting levels did not increase, regulations to mandate voting might be required (see Stapleton and Bates 2002). The response to evidence of opportunism is often a change in laws or regulations, and the most extreme response to opportunism is the association of criminal penalties with a failure to meet prescriptive regulatory requirements. The Sarbanes–Oxley Act of 2002 is a good example in its establishing the responsibility of a firm's managers for internal controls and reporting and in its having sanctions for noncompliance.

If a full separation of ownership and control is the prevailing corporate governance regime in a country having a strong equity market culture, then agency theory suggests that control mechanisms should center on looking after the interests of the shareholders first and foremost. It also suggests that the SRI best-in-class approach to portfolio management, which considers the treatment of stakeholders other than shareholders, may not capture financial outperformance in the context of a pure "agency" regime. This shortcoming may not matter if shareholders are able to operate as a successful control mechanism, but it will depend critically on the structure of ownership. An agency problem in the presence of fragmented ownership would, all other things being equal, be expected to lead to SRI approaches focusing mainly on exclusion (where shareholders might choose to avoid a problem, having no means of influencing it) or, alternatively, shareholder activism (where shareholders might form a coalition and/or take high-profile action to remedy a specific problem).

Stewardship Theory. An alternative view of governance is found in stewardship theory. This view of the world recognizes that money may not be the only effective motivator of managers or employees in a firm. That is, money may be a necessary but insufficient motivator. It may, after a certain point, have more symbolic value than anything else if it acts as a reinforcement of the key motivators of recognition and achievement. Donaldson and Davis (1991) state that in this model, the manager "far from being an opportunistic shirker, . . . wants to be a good steward of the corporate assets" (p. 51). Within this model, it is likely that shareholders view managers as being interested in achieving high performance and capable of using a high level of discretion to act for their benefit, even when they do not own the business and thus do not benefit directly from wealth-creating decisions. In short, managers are likely to identify with the firm sufficiently to behave as if they do benefit directly. The issue in the context of a stewardship regime is, therefore, not to introduce sufficient controls, checks, and balances to control incentives but to structure the organization in such a way that management is able to perform effectively. Regulation that is developed on the basis of stewardship theory is thus likely to take the form of principles and codes (rather than prescriptive regulation). Conversely, such regimes are more likely to prevail in a context in which principles prevail over codes (although which way causality may run is, of course, impossible to prove) because highly prescriptive regulation may well suppress internal value systems.

The best-in-class approach to portfolio management is about identifying firms that perform best with respect to CSR issues, defined as effective handling of environmental, social, and governance risks as they arise in the normal course of business. This approach to social issues is consistent with the identification of firms having a strong internal ethos, requiring the minimum of overt controls, and this description is closest to the stewardship model of corporate governance. If stewardship theory fully explained company governance and performance in the relevant investment context, best-in-class approaches would be the dominant approach to SRI. In the presence of a mix of agency and stewardship regimes, best in class with engagement is likely to be the most prevalent approach to SRI (see also Chapter 3).

Stakeholder Theory. Stakeholder theory holds that corporate management should do right by "labor, suppliers, customers, and owners while simultaneously serving the public interests" (Mason 1958, p. 7).

The issue here is thus to structure the corporation so that a reasonable balance of priorities among shareholders, managers, and other stakeholders is achieved. In the presence of widespread belief in the stakeholder approach, one should expect to find evidence of firms' integrating environmental and social policies with corporate strategy and risk control because the point of the stakeholder approach is the relevance of the wider (social) context. In addition, formal structures may be in place to facilitate dialog between company management and other stakeholders, such as the workforce. For example, codetermination (a feature of the German corporate governance regime established by the 1976 Codetermination Act) denotes the presence of members of the workforce on the company board. One should not be surprised to find stakeholder corporate governance regimes in the context of political regimes that give a fair amount of weight to social issues, and in such regimes, the shareholder or indeed the company manager may possibly weigh less strongly against other stakeholders (such as the workforce or wider society). That is, the predominance of the shareholder is not a given in stakeholder regimes. A criticism of stakeholder regimes is that with so many priorities to balance, they do not resolve the challenge of setting a clear company strategy:

> Unfortunately, proponents of stakeholder theory offer no explanation of how conflicts between different stakeholders are to be resolved. This leaves managers with no principle on which to base decisions, making them accountable to no-one but their own preferences—ironically the very opposite result from that stakeholder theorists hope to achieve. (Jensen 2003, p. 2)

Elsewhere, however, Jensen (2001) discussed the concept of the enlightened stakeholder theory (see Chapter 6), and this approach—in which attention is focused on meeting the needs of the relevant corporate constituencies while accepting value maximization as the firm's objective (e.g., see p. 9)—appears to offer a means of addressing the problem of balancing many priorities.

Stakeholder theory holds that the firm that develops relationships with its stakeholders based on *mutual trust and cooperation* is likely to stand at a competitive advantage relative to others because the costs of monitoring and preventing opportunistic behavior are avoided:

> Firms that solve commitment problems efficiently will have a competitive advantage over those firms that do not. Further, because ethical solutions to commitment problems are more efficient than mechanisms designed to curb opportunism, it follows that firms that contract (through their managers) with their stakeholders on the basis of mutual trust and co-operation will have a competitive advantage over firms that do not. (Jones 1995, p. 422)

In the context of a stakeholder regime well balanced between the relevant counterparties, finding an active best-in-class approach among SRI investors would not be surprising because the stakeholder firm is likely to compete on the basis of environmental and social performance as well as its economic and financial performance. Finding active engagement portfolio approaches would also not be surprising because shareholders in an effectively functioning stakeholder regime would likely speak up on behalf of stakeholders other than themselves. Furthermore, in the context of less-effective stakeholder regimes, one may find that the balance tips so far in the direction of "social" stakeholders that the shareholder ends up with little power. In this case, exclusion and activist portfolios would be likely to prevail in the SRI market. A summary of the SRI approaches and likely corporate governance regimes is found in **Exhibit 2.3**.

At this juncture, it is interesting to note that a body of literature exists on the benefits of investor monitoring. Portfolio risk may be reduced either by diversification or by monitoring firms, or a combination of the two. At the country level, some regimes seem to rely primarily on monitoring (through large blockholders) and others seem to rely primarily on diversification, although in practice, both approaches may be present.[21]

Geographical Trends in Corporate Governance and SRI

This section briefly describes some of the main features of the prevailing corporate governance regime by country, linking this information to the structure of the SRI funds market as described in Chapter 1.

---

[21]See, for example, Porter (1992) and Shleifer and Vishny (1986).

Exhibit 2.3. Summary: Dominant SRI Approach and Corporate Governance Regimes

Dominant Approach	Portfolio Characteristics	Likely Corporate Governance Regime
Exclusion	Return to risk deteriorates in the short run because of reduction in diversification. Pure exclusion portfolios are not constructed with the aim of delivering alpha; the investor is prepared to pay a price to support social beliefs.	Agency problem: Competitive markets do not constrain firms. Stakeholders outside the firm have little power or influence over firms. Alternatively, a stakeholder regime in which shareholders have a lower priority.
Exclusion + best-in-class hybrid	Diversified active portfolio: Under the assumption that manager skill is present, gains from active strategy (portfolio tilted to strong "social" performers) offset by cost of reduced diversification (exclusion).	Agency/stewardship or stakeholder/stewardship. The aim is to find firms having strong internal ethos while avoiding industries in which good stewardship will not address social issues (e.g., see p. 40).
Best in class	Diversified active portfolio strategy with the aim of enhancing performance in the long run.	Stewardship (find firms having the strongest internal ethos) and/or stakeholder (firms compete on financial and CSR criteria).
Best in class + engagement hybrid	Active diversified portfolio with some concentrated positions to permit shareholder to act as owner where relevant. Cost of lower diversification offset by stronger monitoring.	Stewardship (internal ethos)/stakeholder (leverage off ability of external stakeholders to influence company management).
Engagement	Shareholder acts as owner. Risk reduction (and return enhancement) expected to arise from close relationship between shareholder and firm (under the assumption that markets are not strong form efficient) and not from portfolio diversification.	Balanced stakeholder regime/stewardship regime or a combination.
Advocacy	As above.	Agency problem: Competitive markets do not constrain firms. Either a stakeholder regime in which shareholders have a lower priority or an agency regime with heavily fragmented portfolios.

United States. Dispersed ownership and concentrated management, indicating a full separation of ownership and control, appear to characterize the U.S. corporate governance regime. This characterization is captured in two key publications. The first, the well-known book by Berle and Means (2003, originally published in 1932), describes an increasing concentration of power in fewer and fewer managerial hands alongside an "ever-wider dispersion of stock ownership" (p. 47). The second, a 1994 book by Roe, explains the emergence of the so-called Berle–Means corporation in terms of not only economics and technology (the division of labor and specialization) but also politics. He described a policy-driven fragmentation of the ownership of corporations, leaving financial institutions with little scope to "act like an owner." In support of his arguments, he referred to a number of regulations. He noted that ERISA "heightens the legal risks facing a pension manager who is active or takes the big blocks of stocks necessary for activity" (p. 125). He also noted that the fiduciary duty requiring "diligence that…[would be used] in the conduct of an enterprise of a like character and with like aim" (p. 139) makes innovation risky. In Chapter 8, Roe described a number of mutual fund regulations that enforce diversification and penalties for funds that breach diversification rules in the form of the loss of the "pass through" status, resulting in triple taxation.[22] Admati, Pfleiderer, and Zechner (1994) also referred to the prevalence of diversified portfolios. Kinder (2005), however, referred to a new U.S. SEC standard of fiduciary duty that may result in changes in the Roe landscape.

This extremely brief description suggests that, on average, in the United States, the prevailing corporate governance regime is much closer to the agency model than the stakeholder or stewardship models. The reaction to apparent corporate governance failures of the 1990s—externally imposed prescriptive rules with legal sanction for noncompliance (i.e., Sarbanes–Oxley Section 404 and Section 906)—is consistent with the agency model view of the world in which opportunistic behavior is controlled by external mechanisms. But to say that the agency model gives the full picture would be to overstate the case. Voluntary codes can and do become norms. A good example in the area of SRI is the voluntary adoption of Ceres (formerly the Exxon Valdez) Principles by a number of firms (see Appendix A for a listing of the Ceres Principles, Global Sullivan Principles, and UN Global Compact—"The Ten Principles").

Perhaps in response to the apparent imbalance of power between managers and owners in the United States described by Berle and Means (2003) and Roe (1994), a long tradition of shareholder activism has developed in the United States, further propelled in recent years by a reaction to the corporate behavior witnessed during the takeover boom of the 1980s (as described by Monks and Minow 2001) and by corporate-governance-related issues in the aftermath of the technology boom of the 1990s. The number of proxy votes filed in the area of corporate governance and other issues has been growing steadily for some years. This growth trend is described by Romano (2002) as follows: From 1979 to 1983, faith-based groups and a handful of individuals submitted more than half of all proposals; from 1986 until the 1990s, four public pension funds and TIAA-CREF accounted for a fifth of all proposals; from

---

[22]With triple taxation, the firm pays tax on earnings, the fund pays on dividends, and the owner of the fund pays on dividends.

1994 onwards, labor unions overtook public pension funds as the most active sponsors of corporate governance proposals. Elsewhere, Smith (2005) referred to more than 1,100 resolutions on social, environmental, and corporate governance issues in 2004, according to the Investor Responsibility Research Center (IRRC) database.

The U.S. approach to corporate governance can be said to reflect a tradition of agency theory, which views the management of firms as opportunistic and, therefore, allegedly likely to exploit information asymmetries between company management and its shareholders. SRI approaches to portfolio management implemented in the context of such a tradition are likely to focus mainly on exclusion and, of course, shareholder activism. This characterization appears, at least on the basis of this very superficial analysis, to describe the SRI market in the United States.

United Kingdom. In the United Kingdom, the essence of the current corporate governance system is captured in Section 1.1 of the 1992 Cadbury Report from the Cadbury Committee, which asserts that boards "must be free to drive their companies forward but exercise that freedom within a reasonable framework of accountability" (p. 1).[23] Economic success is the primary function of firms but not without regard to the context that they operate in. Equally essential to U.K. corporate governance is the so-called comply or explain approach with respect to the principles and rules relating to corporate accountability—see, for example, the introduction to the Combined Code on Corporate Governance (FSA 2003). There is a consistent recognition that shareholders must be the prime mover or main stakeholder—see OFR Reporting Standard 1 (ASB 2005) and Chapter 4 of this monograph for more detail. A precursor of the current Combined Code, the final report issued by the Hampel Committee in January 1998, however, observes that good governance ensures that all stakeholders with a relevant interest in the firm's business are fully taken into account. The main principles of the Combined Code include not only the separation of chair and chief executive, a well-balanced board, remuneration linked to corporate and individual performance, a sound system of internal controls, and transparent, objective reporting and audit systems but also a dialog with shareholders based on mutual understanding of objectives. Section II of the Combined Code focuses on the duties and responsibilities of shareholders— namely, dialog and considered use of the shareholder vote.

The principles-based comply or explain approach to corporate governance has some of the hallmarks of a stewardship approach in that the board is given the freedom to work as the members collectively see fit. The recognition that constituencies with a relevant interest in the business should be taken into account is clearly about stakeholders. Nevertheless, many of the specific principles of the Combined Code listed in the previous paragraph are mechanisms designed to address the

---

[23]Note that the U.K. system has changed quite considerably since the 1970s, when the presence of very large stakes suggested that ownership and control were not separate for many firms. See Cheffins (2002).

agency problem. In this regard, Section 1.7 of the final report issued by the Hampel Committee (1998) notes that the Cadbury Report and the Greenbury Report (both fully incorporated in the Combined Code) were responses to what could be described as opportunism in the form of corporate failures and allegedly unjustified compensation packages, respectively. Although elements of both stewardship and stakeholder approaches exist in U.K. corporate governance codes, the need to balance the rights and responsibilities of managers and owners—the agency problem—is a consistent keynote throughout. Overall, the main features of the corporate governance regime as briefly described here make it unsurprising that the SRI market in the United Kingdom should be particularly active in the best-in-class and engagement strategies, and combinations of the two, alongside traditional SRI exclusion funds. SRI as practiced in the United Kingdom thus appears to reflect, and may have been shaped by, developments in the corporate governance regime.

France. The French system of corporate governance is often described in the corporate governance literature—such as McCahery, Moerland, Raajimakers, and Renneboog (2002)—as an "insider" or blockholder system. Ownership is characterized by concentrated stakes, and these stakes often take the form of corporate cross-holdings, as described in Franks and Mayer (1997). Thus, block shareholders exert a strong monitoring influence. But because French board members are often drawn from the network of corporations that are also likely to hold controlling stakes, in practice, little outside influence may be in place. Minority shareholders, sitting outside this networking system, are likely to have relatively little power. In the late 1990s, France, along with other countries, published corporate governance codes. Viénot 2 recommends choice with respect to separation or otherwise of the roles of CEO and chairman of the board; transparency with respect to director compensation, including stock options; a four-year limit to director terms of employment; independent directors be at least one-third of the board and also of the audit and appointments committees; and a timely reporting cycle. Although these recommendations are in the spirit of those seen earlier in the context of U.K. codes, they are unlikely to translate to a similar relationship between management and shareholders. Viénot 1 says: "the director represents the collective body of shareholders and must act, at all times, in the interests of the firm as an organizational, or organic, whole" (Viénot Report 1995, p. 21).[24]

This belief is, in spirit, quite different from the emphasis on the shareholder in the corporate governance codes of market-based, rather than blockholder, systems (such as in the United States and the United Kingdom). The French corporate

---

[24] "Bien qu'etant lui-meme actionnaire, l'administrateur represente l'ensemble des actionnaires et doit agir en toutes circonstances dans l'interet social de l'entreprise." With thanks to Philippe Tibi of UBS for his advice on the translation.

          ©2006, The Research Foundation of CFA Institute

governance code includes recommendations typically designed to resolve the agency problem, such as the independent director requirement. The thinking underlying Viénot, however, appears to be more closely aligned with stakeholder theory.

Overall, France appears to be characterized by a stakeholder corporate governance regime in which the influence of the minority shareholder is reduced by the "insider" nature of the system. Against this background, one would expect to find mainly exclusion portfolios in the SRI market, with engagement largely taking the form of shareholder activism. One would not expect to find much best-in-class portfolio management, and the surprise in France is that best in class is, in fact, an active segment. Why? One clue may be provided by some of the specific features of the French SRI market described in Chapter 1. Best-in-class investment may turn out to have an impact similar to activist approaches when implemented by a cohort!

Germany. The corporate governance system in Germany is also described in the literature (e.g., in McCahery, Moerland, Raajimakers, and Renneboog 2002), as an "insider" system. Block holdings have traditionally been common (as in France), and in Germany, voting rights can also be separated from cash flow rights. The distinguishing feature of corporate governance in Germany is the role played by banks in relationship to firms and their governance. Several writers on corporate governance refer to the control over firms allegedly gained by German banks through the use of the proxy voting system. As Roe (1994) wrote, "In Germany, banks enter boardrooms by combining votes from stock they own directly, stock in bank-controlled investment companies, and stock they hold only as broker but also vote" (p. 170). From an SRI perspective, it is significant that the involvement of German banks in governance is likely to be rooted in social policy. One function of bank ownership traditionally may have been to influence firms in the direction of government policy. Social and environmental issues may well be dealt with via government policy rather than proactively by firms. Although the German Corporate Governance Code, as amended 2 June 2005 (see Commission of the German Corporate Governance Code 2005), focuses on recommendations likely to address the agency problem (such as one share one vote, pre-emptive rights, the right of a quorum of shareholders to demand a meeting, disclosure of board compensation, the independence of the audit committee, disclosure of changes in significant stakes, and principles for reporting and disclosure), some features contrast with other regimes. A dual board structure working on the basis of a cooperative relationship between supervisory and management boards is required by law for German stock companies, and codetermination (employees represented on the board) is required for firms larger than a given size.

In very broad terms, one could say that the German corporate governance system is a stakeholder system in which some shareholders (blockholders), institutions (banks), and other stakeholders (employees) have considerable influence but in which minority shareholders may not. In a stakeholder system with a bias away from the minority shareholder, one would expect SRI funds to be primarily exclusion funds. The engagement role of shareholders is taken up fully inside the system. Therefore, minority shareholders are likely to be passive, or if the need arises, they are likely to engage in activism to have their voices heard. These conditions may help explain why the SRI market is relatively low profile in Germany, as described in Chapter 1.

The Netherlands. As described by De Jong, Kabir, Marra, and Röell (2001, p. 198), in Holland, the "structure regime" takes to an extreme the separation of ownership from control, ensuring a concentration of control within the firm. Ownership (by minority shareholders) without the right to vote is contrived by having a trustee office of the company hold shares in exchange for depositary certificates that give the owner the right to dividends and to attend (also call) shareholder meetings but no right to vote. The Peters Committee (in its 1997 report on corporate governance) questions the structure regime on the basis of the increasing internationalization of the shareholder base of Dutch companies. Therefore, the report's 40 recommendations and changing expectations with respect to the role of the shareholder focus on the independence of directors and related issues, such as remuneration, the role of shareholders, and the significance of the shareholder vote, including the need for an efficient proxy system. Nevertheless, Dutch corporate governance clearly remains based on a stakeholder system in which the shareholder may not always be the top priority. The firm in the Netherlands is:

> a long-term collaboration between the various parties involved, [namely] . . . employees, shareholders, . . . suppliers and customers, but also governments and civil society.[25] (*Dutch Corporate Governance Code*, 2003, p. 3)

Under this code, the continuity of the firm, therefore, its *long term* return on capital, is an important priority. The two boards (management and supervisory) "should take account of the interests of different stakeholders" according to *The Dutch Corporate Governance Code* (p. 3). Overall, the Netherlands appears to be a good example of a stakeholder regime in which the shareholder cannot rely on being the lead stakeholder. These brief details on Dutch corporate governance, therefore, suggest that SRI funds are likely to be predominantly exclusion funds with shareholder engagement, if any, likely to take the form of activism. There appears to be little opportunity for shareholder engagement in the context of a full structure regime, and for shareholders wishing to communicate with firms, activism may be the only available route unless evolving corporate governance codes change the landscape.

---

[25]The requirement that Dutch boards should protect the company as a whole also appears in the Dutch Civil Code, Book 2, Sections 140.2 and 250.2 (as footnoted by Moerland 2002).

Japan. Japan's corporate governance system is often compared with Germany's "universal bank" approach. A firm's main lenders also tend to be shareholders, and historically, bank-led groupings of firms (i.e., the *keiretsu* system, which has been in decline since the mid-1980s) created groups of closely affiliated companies. As key stakeholders, the lending banks are in a position to monitor and control firms closely, although this situation may be changing owing to the restructuring of the banking sector. Japan's governance system could be described as a stakeholder system in the sense that a number of interest groups have traditionally been involved in monitoring and controlling corporations—as described, for example, by Ozawa (2000). It has also traditionally been an "insider" system through the well-known network of cross holdings, although this is weakening. It is thus unsurprising to find that generating profit for the shareholder has traditionally been a "secondary objective" (Sakuma 2001). Ozawa (2000) also stated that shareholder activism in Japan is "sporadic and ineffective." Social and environmental concerns in Japan have, therefore, tended to be centrally managed and at times in a way that may not always be inclusive of some stakeholders, such as small and medium-sized enterprises.[26] Japan's governance system appears to be in transition, which may be one stimulus for the nascent SRI market.

Summary

Overall, corporate governance regimes vary considerably from one country to the next. They are shaped by the relative social importance of financial markets and contribute to the shaping of approaches to SRI. Corporate governance regimes are critical as a balancing mechanism between stakeholders, and how they work will, almost inevitably, have an influence on the distribution of the benefits and costs of economic activity, as well as the cash flows.

The key point to emerge from Chapter 2 is perhaps that the assumptions underlying some of the ancillary disciplines commonly applied in the process of portfolio management have shaped the relationship between the finance industry and society in the specific context in which they are based. In particular, the assumptions of the efficient market hypothesis appear to run through many of the disciplines that inform investment practices—economics, corporate governance, accounting, valuation, and portfolio construction. As hopefully will become clear in later chapters, however, the four main approaches to SRI identified in this monograph are based on a rejection of efficiency somewhere in the system.

---

[26]With thanks to Paul Donovan for making this interesting comment.

3. Main Stakeholders in SRI

The successful alignment of the interests of the many stakeholders affected by any form of economic activity—society, future generations, consumers, the corporation, shareholders and other investors, markets, and governments—is a prerequisite for economic success over the medium term. If any single stakeholder either enjoys disproportionate benefits or suffers disproportionate costs in relation to any economic activity, then the balance may need to be redressed. This change can be driven by one or more of several interest groups or social institutions as seen in Chapters 1 and 2—governments or regulators, markets, industry bodies, shareholder groups, or activists—and sometimes by a combination of several of them, depending on the specific circumstances.

As mentioned in the Preface, the field of social responsibility can be framed as the management of potential conflicts of interest between different societal groups, or stakeholders, with respect to economic, environmental, social, and ethical issues. A conflict of interest can occur when economic or commercial activity that is good for one party is not in the best interests of others. SRI conflicts from the realm of commerce include an economic or business activity in which a side effect is one or more of the following: pollution of the environment; the power of large firms to put extreme pricing pressure on firms in their supply chain or to suppress the wages of employees below reasonable levels or (because it is not a one-way street) the power of suppliers or employees to extract more than a fair price in exchange for products, work, or other services delivered; the ability of owners of scarce resources to extract more than a "reasonable" rent; the creation of unresolved dilemmas over the right duration of pharmaceutical patents with respect to drugs needed by poorer communities; and the emergence of social divides created by the ability (or inability) to afford access to certain goods and services, such as food, heating and light, communications services, or financial services.

The two key perspectives on social responsibility for the purposes of, and within the purview of, this monograph are the corporate perspective and the investor perspective. So, the main discussion in this chapter is on the interaction between the corporation and the other stakeholders in the business with a particular, but not exclusive, concentration on the investor as a stakeholder, which means financial considerations are firmly in focus. It does not mean that financial stakeholders are necessarily the most important stakeholders; it simply reflects the context in which this monograph is written.

 ©2006, The Research Foundation of CFA Institute

Financial Performance and Other Stakeholder Interests

For the firm, corporate social responsibility is about the firm's relationship with relevant stakeholders. For the investor, socially responsible investment is an approach in which the relevant fiduciary seeks to invest in such a way as to minimize or otherwise control the risk of investment exposure to the aforementioned conflicts of interest and their consequences, which, of course, can be financial as well as purely environmental, social, or ethical. For financial analysts in general, the way in which firms interact with other stakeholders can provide valuable information about the overall risk profile of the debt and equity of individual firms or indeed entire sectors.

The stakeholder question is not the exclusive territory of the socially responsible investment specialty. After all, how the firm relates to its customers, labor force, suppliers, regulators, and the government is likely to have a strong influence on its economic success, which, of course, includes its profitability as well as performance in CSR areas. Conversely, the economic success of a firm, including its profitability, is likely to have a strong influence on the way it interacts with its other stakeholders from all perspectives—including environmental, social, and ethical impacts. Just as cash-constrained firms may be precluded from making long-term investments in all areas of the business (capital investment, brand building, R&D, environmental controls, health and safety, and human capital development), so too strong cash generators would be expected to invest as required by the overall business. Whereas cash-constrained firms might be expected to focus mainly on suppliers of funding (shareholders, lenders), cash-rich firms would have greater freedom to take a more-balanced, and longer-term, perspective, encompassing more than one or two financial stakeholders. Empirical evidence has been found to support this argument in the context of pollution control:

> Financial ability appears to play an important role in environmental performance. Firms in more concentrated industries and with higher cash flows tend to be lower baseline emitters of toxic chemicals. Further, firms with more constrained cash flow positions are more likely to increase their TRI emissions (or reduce less) relative to their industry peers over time. (Konar and Cohen 2000, p. 29)

Of course, the reverse can hold too: The U.S. EPA has observed that advantages gained by noncompliance with environmental laws can include gains in market share, revenue gains from selling products or services prohibited by law, operations begun ahead of competitors by being prior to regulatory approval, and higher operating capacity gain by one firm at the expense of others (EPA 2003, p. 5). Which alternative prevails—competing on the basis of best-in-class performance or joining the "race to the bottom"—may depend on which strategic choice was made by the (hypothetical) firm. Any corporate strategy that does not *knowingly* incorporate the relevant environmental, social, and ethical issues together with economic and financial ones is incomplete. Thus, social responsibility would appear to be inevitably integral to corporate strategy, and the extent to which this is (or is not) the case for individual firms is likely to be a relevant input to all analysts assessing the merits of specific stocks for the investment portfolio.

The general idea put forth by the title of Friedman's 1970 article, "The Social Responsibility of Business Is to Increase Its Profits," is compelling in its simplicity, which may explain why it is so often quoted! After all, charities and foundations have to be run on a financially sound basis, balanced with strategic objectives. But as the previous paragraph suggested, a focus on the bottom line to the exclusion of other relevant environmental, social, governance, or ethical considerations (which tends to mean the "accounting" bottom line in the relatively short run) is unlikely to be how the best run firms operate simply because they can afford to take a strategic perspective. This infamous phrase of Friedman's, in fact, begs as many questions as it answers as soon as the role of the firm is considered in real life and in the context of its many relationships. Clearly, a number of conditions may need to be added to Friedman's phrase, such as a definition of "profit," a time horizon, and of course, a set of governing values.

Corporate Governance: The Firm and Its Stakeholders

The extent to which corporate social responsibility is managed as an integral part of corporate strategy is likely to come down to the corporate governance environment of individual firms. If the social responsibility of firms is to increase profits, few investors are likely to disagree that it needs to be within reasonable constraints. This concept—that profit should be generated within a reasonable framework of accountability—is perhaps best illustrated in **Exhibit 3.1**, a summary of the Cadbury perspective on corporate governance found in the Cadbury report (Cadbury Committee 1992).

Exhibit 3.1. Corporate Governance and Social Responsibility According to Cadbury, United Kingdom

Cadbury Level	Cadbury Definition	Relevant Framework
Level 1	Material obligations to shareholders, employees, customers, suppliers, creditors, taxation, and legal duties.	Financial statements, contract terms, competition and finance law, regulation, measurement, reporting.
Level 2	The direct results of the actions of a firm on the human capital of a community, on the environment.	Corporate strategy and beliefs: minimize adverse consequences of actions.
Level 3	Maintaining the framework of the society in which it operates, reflecting society's priorities in addition to its own commercial ones.	Intangible controls: company ethos (envisage wider consequences of decisions and build awareness into decision-making process).

Source: Based on definitions of social responsibility in Cadbury (2002, p. 160–161.)

 ©2006, The Research Foundation of CFA Institute

The stakeholders named in Levels 2 and 3 in this scheme may appear to be primarily relevant to the SRI and CSR specialists. But if the three levels are not fully integrated, a problem of some sort at Level 2 or 3 can quickly become a Level 1 problem. For example, the maintenance of the "framework of society in which it operates" can be interpreted to include the financial markets and product markets that the firm relies on to raise capital and distribute its products. (Such markets are important to the firm but also external to the firm, and many stakeholders quite far removed from the firm rely on them, directly or indirectly.) Most investors can probably remember instances of damage done to financial and other markets by the very firms that rely on them. Without the relevant market infrastructure in place, the net present value of the firm's future cash flows might be severely reduced no matter how good the firm is individually and the viability of firms in the relevant market compromised even in the short run. This situation would clearly not be positive for many stakeholders (not just the shareholders but also firms' suppliers, employees, and customers, to name a few); therefore, including stewardship of the marketplace among the corporate governance concerns of the firm would seem reasonable. Given the potential significance of this addition in both financial and social terms, the relationship between the firm and its major market "microstructures" is something all analysts, whether generalist or SRI specialist, are likely to find useful when assessing the risk profile of the firm's debt or equity.

As observed in Chapter 2, the corporate governance framework of the firm is, in more general terms, responsible for making sure that reasonable balance is maintained between stakeholders. Note that the use of Exhibit 3.1 is not intended to suggest that U.K. corporate governance is always the ideal approach. As seen in the previous chapter, the role played by the firm within society varies from one country to another. The generation of profit for shareholders may be a secondary concern in some strongly stakeholder jurisdictions. In other regimes, firms tend to be held in the hands of a family (Italy) or a controlling group (Scandinavia). For the lead shareholders, ownership and control are arguably not separated. In such situations, for whom is profit generated? The answer depends very much on the incentives of those in the controlling group, and these individuals may have very different interests at heart depending on the context in which they are operating. Hence, the ideal approach to governance (and the point at which the Level 2 and 3 concerns are handled) may be different from one country to the next.

The key point is that the way a firm handles environmental, social, and ethical issues is likely to be shaped by the firm's corporate governance practices; therefore, from the perspective of the investor (whether generalist or SRI specialist) as a stakeholder, the positioning of the firm with respect to all relevant stakeholders (and not the shareholder in isolation) is likely to provide an informative window into the firm's strategic direction and risk control.

Regulation: How It Relates to the Firm's Stakeholders

Sometimes, a firm's internal controls may not be sufficient to deal with some conflicts of interest because the problem is pervasive to the industry or the market, and dealing with it unilaterally might, in fact, create a nonlevel competitive playing field in which the first mover toward good practice is penalized. In such situations, it is sometimes possible for an industry to deal with issues as a body. A current example is the ACEA Agreement, a voluntary agreement by the European Automobile Manufacturers Association and the European Commission to reduce carbon dioxide (CO_2) emission rates of passenger vehicles sold in the European Union to a fleet average of 140 grams of CO_2 per kilometer by 2008. As Sauer, Mettler, Wellington, and Grab Hartmann (2005) observe, if the industry fails to meet the 2008 target, the commission is expected to adopt formal regulations to reduce CO_2 emissions from new passenger vehicles.

A particularly useful concept in this context is the planning balance sheet, a concept also explored in Hudson (2005)—first developed in the context of urban planning in the United Kingdom in the 1950s and 1960s.[27] By drawing on the balance sheet concept, any economic activity can be viewed as a series of transactions between "producers," "operators," and "consumers" in goods and services and other "social" resources. In the context of CSR, incorporating distributional effects into an analysis of corporate activity is likely to throw light on the extent to which the distribution of costs and benefits might be skewed among managers, owners, suppliers, the labor force, consumers, the government sector, the wider community, and future generations. The presence of an asset (or benefit) belonging to one party that is offset by a liability (or cost) accruing to another could be interpreted as a social, or stakeholder, balance sheet.

This concept is shown in **Exhibit 3.2** as a hypothetical example for climate change. In the presence of climate change caused by greenhouse gas emissions, and with no policy in place, costs and benefits might be described as shown in the exhibit. With a policy in place—such as the EU Emissions Trading Scheme—some of the benefits become costs as the costs of CO_2 emission become financial. So, translated by the fact that with the Emissions Trading Scheme in place, CO_2 has a price. As a consequence, some of the benefits of not acting may become costs in the short run rather than remaining in the very long run; however, some of the costs of not acting (mostly latent) may or may not be reduced. The potential benefits of acting to mitigate global warming are unknown, which may be seen as a reason not to sustain avoidance or mitigation costs in the present day. But if numbers were put into the columns in Exhibit 3.2, the potential scale of risk to the community would be a powerful argument for taking action, even if success were not assured.

---

[27]A balance sheet approach to handle distribution effects was explained by Lichfield in 1956, as referenced in Lichfield, Kettle, and Whitbread (1975, p. 78).

    ©2006, The Research Foundation of CFA Institute

Exhibit 3.2. Hypothetical Climate Change Stakeholder Balance Sheet Assuming No CO$_2$ Trading

Stakeholder	Benefit	Cost
Management	Compensation unaffected by emissions not avoided.	Latent reputational cost. See also community—potential liabilities.
Employees	Compensation unaffected by emissions not avoided.	May have no choice as to CO$_2$ profile of products or services. Environmental costs sustained as community member.
Competing peer group of firms	Depends on market structure.	Depends on market structure.
Shareholders	Return on capital and pricing of equity unaffected by emissions not avoided.	Latent financial risk. Costs sustained as community member.
Lenders	Emissions not avoided (cost saved).	Latent financial risk. Costs sustained as community member.
Suppliers	Emissions not avoided.	Potential disruption to business in the context of associated environmental change.
Customers	Emissions not avoided.	Costs sustained as community member.
Community	Cheaper transport (mitigation cost avoided).	Emissions and associated pollution.
Government	Tax revenues unaffected by emissions not avoided.	Potential future "fire fighting" in the context of associated environmental change.

Note: This concept was first explored in the context of Hudson (2005).

Finally, the key point for firms is that, in the presence of policy action, such as CO$_2$ trading, the competitive playing field is likely to change, making it possible for firms to compete to be best in class in terms of their greenhouse gas footprint.

Exhibit 3.3 gives several other examples and summarizes typical social concerns, together with potential financial implications for the firm. Several of the issues listed are well known and fully regulated where markets or self-regulation were not sufficient to address the conflict of interest between the key stakeholders in each case. In every case, the impact of the issue on the firm (or sometimes the firm on the issue) is likely to be shaped by corporate strategy in the context of the relevant industry structure.

Competition and the Firm's Stakeholders

A firm's internal controls and values (its corporate governance) together with external controls, such as regulation, are likely to determine how conflicts of interest between stakeholders play out. In addition, the structure of an industry may have a

Exhibit 3.3. Stakeholders, Issues, and Financial Relevance: Examples

Context	SRI Issue	Financial Issue
Environmental pollution	Avoidance or cleanup?	Cost of weak operational controls as reflected in poor environmental control. Cleanup costs and other penalties. Costs of investing in pollution control. If pollution avoided, benefit of more efficient operations, benefit of upgrading systems.
Concentrated market	Unfair price to consumer? Market sustainable (or not) as a monopoly/oligopoly?	Unsustainable supernormal profits?
Supply-chain structure: many small suppliers	Fair treatment of supplier?	Impact from potential supply-chain disruption? How likely?
Labor force	Fair treatment of labor force: health and safety, training, collective bargaining, and so on?	Productivity, adaptability, continuity, and so on.
Scarce resources	Access rights?	Price of access. Security of raw material supply.
R&D, sufficient protection of property rights?	Social needs (e.g., drug needs for developing countries) addressed in the R&D agenda?	Reasonable returns on investment in R&D? Regulatory or political risk arising from social issues relating to the firm's intellectual capital?
Brand building	Use of advertising within reasonable constraints?	Reasonable returns on investment in advertising? Regulatory risks? Regulatory risks handled adequately within the business model?
Universal access requirement	Universal access adequately handled?	Regulatory requirements permit firms to earn a reasonable return on capital?

bearing not only on the profitability of an industry and companies within it but also, of course, on its environmental, social, and ethical performance. Put another way:

> Unless environmental [social, governance, and ethical] issues are dealt with inside the corporation in ways similar to those used to manage other business risks and opportunities, environmental control [and the handling of other social, governance, and ethical issues] in such industries will remain an internal regulatory function superimposed on the company's core business concerns rather than part of the process of maximizing shareholder value. (Repetto and Austin 2000, p. 1)[28]

---

[28]The authors reference Smart (1992).

©2006, The Research Foundation of CFA Institute

Most financial analysts are familiar with the five forces of the Porter analysis. The social dimension of the Porter approach, and the relevance of the social dimension to finance, is usually no more than a subtext in most analysis. And yet, the Porter framework can be said to encapsulate the dynamic between the major stakeholders in the corporation. Porter and Van der Linde (1995b) described the link between competition and environmental performance in their often-cited article "Toward a New Conception of the Environment," in which innovative "product" and "process" offsets are described. The following paragraphs give examples of links between the five competitive forces and social issues, extending the argument beyond purely environmental issues.

1. Industry Competitors—Rivalry among Existing Firms. Firms jockey for position within a particular market or industry. The number of players and the competitive strategies and tactics used in the industry are likely to determine industry profitability, on average, and firm profitability within the industry. The social consequences of some forms of competition are well recognized within competition law, although when to intervene may not always be clear. Firms can and do compete to perform in the context of environmental or social issues. For example, Konar and Cohen (2000) observed that firms in the United States have dramatically reduced many of the toxic chemicals released into the air, water, and soil despite the fact that no laws or regulations required these reductions. The authors commented that:

> Assuming this fact cannot be explained solely on the basis of altruistic behavior, firms must be acting in profit maximizing ways when determining it is in their own self interest to reduce pollution beyond any legally mandated level. There are many possible sources of benefits to a firm wishing to voluntarily reduce emissions beyond compliance, including: better public and community relations, reduced costs and higher productivity due to better utilization of chemical resources and other production inputs, better employee morale, improved firm reputation with con-sumers, and reduced threat of citizen lawsuit. (Konar and Cohen 2000, p. 28)

2. Bargaining Power of Suppliers. If a large firm deals with many suppliers, the bargaining power of the buyer will likely be far greater than that of a smaller firm facing one or two large suppliers, and this situation is likely to affect relative competitive strength and (ultimately) the profitability of firms depending on their relative positioning. When assessing the relative merits of firms from a financial perspective, the strength of supply-chain relationships is something the analyst may take into account with respect to short-run performance. Less often taken into account, but no less relevant, are the social consequences of aggressive supply-chain management by firms. A dominant firm may inadvertently foreclose access to the supply chain to others, may compromise the financial viability of firms in the supply chain, may compromise the quality of goods, or may not take sufficient account of the human rights of employees within the supply chain. Society may push back through the mechanisms of antitrust or competitive product markets or through nongovernment organizations (NGOs) or other lobbying groups. If this push back happens, it may directly affect the firm's business model and, therefore, potentially the firm's profitability.

3. Bargaining Power of Customers. If a firm has a fragmented customer base or one that is in some way captive, it is clearly relevant to finance because the structure of a firm's customer base, as well as the way it is handled by the firm, can influence profitability. Potential social consequences may also exist: A captive customer base may not have free choice with respect to certain consumer products, for instance. The financial analyst may believe this situation to be irrelevant or, indeed, may view a captive customer base as enhancing earnings quality. But consumers who are unable to take their business elsewhere may look for other ways of expressing their preferences, which is simply another way of saying that if competitive markets cannot solve the problem (for customers), regulation or the law may come into the picture, increasing business risk (and potentially reducing earnings quality or predictability).

4. Substitutes—Threat of New Products or Services. In the context of environmental performance, product or process offsets are particularly relevant: New environmental regulations may trigger innovation in such a way as to supplant firms' key markets. Elsewhere, if technological development is critical to the competitive strength of a firm, the ability of the firm to earn returns to R&D (or sometimes simply to cover the costs) will depend on the competitive structure of the industry as well as the competence of the firm itself in attaching revenue and profit to research effort. But this is widely recognized (by financial analysts) not to be the whole story. Social issues are particularly relevant, and well recognized, in the context of technological advance. The strength of the legal protection of intellectual property rights in context could, for instance, have a direct impact on profitability, as may the way in which research processes and patents are regulated. Changes in these areas can be critical to trends in company profitability and, therefore, are routinely watched by financial analysts in technology, media, and pharmaceuticals sectors, for example. Similarly, product risk (side effects in the drugs markets, for instance, or new products that fail in some way and have to be recalled) is well recognized.

5. Potential Entrants. When markets change, it may give scope for new entrants to the market. The resolution of some stakeholder issues may give rise to completely new ways of doing things, and new ways of doing things often bring new entrants to an industry because they require innovation. A current good example may be the increasing number of initiatives taken by governments and other stakeholders to mitigate the risk of climate change arising from the burning of fossil fuels. It is too soon to say what impact such initiatives may have on the overall structure of the energy market; however, alternative energy technologies are examples of actual and potential new entrants.

Summary. Although an analysis of competitive conditions can help highlight potential externalities (and, therefore, issues that may be relevant to socially responsible investment) there would appear to be no guarantees that incorporating CSR issues within a firm's corporate strategy will always lead to superior returns. Commentary by Esty and Porter (1998) made this situation clear through an effective parallel. The field of industrial ecology is about the impact of designing for eco-efficiency (for instance, within the production process) in such a way as to enhance competitiveness. Esty and Porter (p. 35) commented that, in particular, if the regulatory playing field is not even, environmentally responsible firms may end up with a cost disadvantage; see also Chapter 2.

The Shareholder and the Firm's Other Stakeholders

Finance, regulation, the firm's internal controls and values—all play a part in determining the way potential conflicts of interest between a firm's stakeholders play out. Last, but absolutely not least, is the owner. The shareholder, as a fiduciary, has an extremely important and influential role to play in shaping the balance of interests between stakeholders. Exactly how this role plays out will vary from one country to another, depending critically on the prevailing corporate governance environment, which, as shown, will determine whether investors attempt to influence firms primarily through exclusion policies, engagement, or activism. Konar and Cohen (2000, p. 28) noted that the visibility of the largest firms in financial markets may also have acted as a powerful incentive. When social issues become priced in markets, it can change company behavior. In a 1997 study examining the effects of stock price reductions on firm behavior, Konar and Cohen found that firms that received a significant stock price reduction upon disclosing their TRI (toxics release inventory) emissions subsequently reduced their emissions more than their industry peers, even if their industry peers had higher levels of emissions to begin with.

With respect to many environmental and social issues, it is the interaction between markets, regulation, corporate firm managers, and firm owners that determines how social and environmental costs and benefits are distributed, which will, in turn, affect the return and risk profile of most assets and liabilities. In this sense, no investor can avoid social issues. Investment decision making, in a general sense, is inescapably involved in assessing social issues. In its narrowest sense, the financial imperative for SRI is, simply, that environmental, social, ethical, and governance issues often crystallize. Finance is, however, just one perspective on the much broader issue of economic value added, which can and does incorporate intangibles. Leveraging the technological, operational, commercial, and financial skills of companies in such a way as to create value (in the broadest sense—economic, financial, environmental, and social) is the real imperative for CSR.

Summary

The field of social responsibility can be framed as the management of potential conflicts of interest between different societal groups, or stakeholders with respect to economic, environmental, social, and ethical issues. For the firm, corporate social responsibility is about its relationship with relevant stakeholders. For the investor, socially responsible investment is an approach in which the relevant fiduciary seeks to invest in such a way as to minimize or otherwise control the risk of investment exposure to the aforementioned potential conflicts of interest and their consequences. The extent to which corporate social responsibility is managed as an integral part of corporate strategy by firms is likely to come down to the corporate governance environment of individual firms, which means that some corporate governance frameworks may be a useful input to analysis but with some adjustment for the jurisdiction in which the analysis is applied.

Corporate governance is not likely to be enough as an analytical input in isolation: The structure of an industry can have a bearing not only on the profitability of an industry and companies within it but also, of course, on their environmental, social, and ethical performance and on the extent to which a regulatory overlay may be needed to redress the balance between stakeholders. In this context, the Porter competitive framework together with the "stakeholder balance sheet" may be useful analytical tools.

Finally, the shareholder, as a fiduciary, has an important role to play in shaping the balance of interests between stakeholders. The functioning of the financial sector will shape how this role works in practice. In any market system, it could be said that that it is the social responsibility of the financial sector to link social issues to finance where it is reasonable and feasible to do so and, of course, within a reasonable framework of accountability. The reasonable framework of accountability means it is also important to recognize when it is neither feasible nor reasonable to connect finance to social issues, which is, essentially, when ethics or value systems must prevail.

          ©2006, The Research Foundation of CFA Institute

4. Disclosure and Reporting

From the point of view of financial analysts, the ideal accounting regime would be sufficiently consistent to make companies comparable within industries and through time—or as Black wrote: "We want that set of accounting rules that makes prices earnings ratios most nearly constant, both across firms and across time" (1980, p. 19).

To attain this goal, what is needed is a set of accounting rules that would permit analysts to draw up a reasonably accurate picture of the economic earnings of firms.[29] In an ideal world, the complete picture of economic earnings would, according to Henriques and Richardson (2004, p. 3), incorporate all dimensions of economic value added, including environmental and social value added or destroyed—benefits or costs generated in the course of business and often "externalized" by many conventional reporting systems but nevertheless relevant to long-term value creation.

Accounting concepts tend to develop over time in response to need. In particular, a reaction to the aftermath of the technology bubble of the late 1990s is an increasing awareness of the need for companies to disclose information that permits a longer-term perspective:

> While corporations cannot indicate how investors make their decisions, they can provide them with information that is focused more on long-term strategies, financial goals, and intrinsic values, and less on transitory short-term factors. Corporations should re-evaluate the implications of providing short-term earnings guidance as well as the advisability of meeting financial targets through aggressive accounting techniques. (Conference Board Commission on Public Trust and Private Enterprise 2003, p. 34)

Whereas, historically, perhaps one or two key stakeholders—the tax authorities, the bank or other lenders, or the shareholder, depending on the country—were the target audience of financial statements, currently, the readership of financial statements is much wider and extends to a broader number of stakeholders, including the broader market, customers, suppliers, the workforce, nongovernment organizations, and the general public. Hence:

> The way we'd teach accounting five years ago was mostly from the standpoint of how this information helps the analyst value the firm. But [this] has been altered to recognize the first order of governance—this is your view into the company. It is the fundamental mechanism through which the public and markets are able to monitor what's going on. (Robert Bushman, as quoted in the *Financial Times* 4 October 2004)

---

[29] The concept of EVA (economic value added) probably gets closest to this ideal, but it is unlikely that sufficient information is in the public domain for analysts to calculate a firm's EVA from an outside perspective.

The increasing importance of stakeholders other than the shareholder is apparent in some reporting guidelines, too. For instance, the General Guidelines on Environmental Reporting issued by DEFRA (United Kingdom) discuss not only which firms should report on their environmental impacts, and how, but also, to whom such reports may be of interest—naming employees; suppliers of goods and services; customers; funders/shareholders and other investors including bankers and insurers; government including regulators, local and planning authorities; academics/commentators including relevant pressure groups; local community and neighbors. (DEFRA 2001, para 2.1)

Currently, reporting on environmental, social, ethical, and governance issues tends to be voluntary unless the law requires disclosure or, alternatively, unless an imminent and significant potential financial impact can be identified, in which case environmental or social costs or benefits (losses or gains) would be expected to appear within conventional accounting frameworks as financial items. Regulatory change sometimes brings about such accounting changes. In several countries, for instance, trading schemes are used to deal with hazardous emissions, such as the U.S. cap and trade scheme for NO_x (nitrogen oxides) and SO_x (sulfurous oxides, or acid rain) emissions[30] and the Emissions Trading Scheme in Europe for CO_2.[31] These regulatory changes put a price on emissions, and accounting rules then tend to be developed to determine how the effects of the regulation should be valued in company accounts.

Sometimes, changes in corporate governance regimes may be the trigger for reporting changes. Changes to related laws, regulations, or codes in the United States (such as the Sarbanes–Oxley Act) and Europe (such as the U.K. Combined Code on Corporate Governance) are likely to have two influences: (1) The way corporate governance is practiced and reported on is likely to change, and (2) because corporate governance links directly to the internal controls of a firm, affecting, in turn, what is monitored and reported, broader indirect effects on company reports are also likely to be evident. Although the main focus of many corporate governance codes is the relationship between shareholders and management, some European codes, such as the Dutch Corporate Governance Code, also refer to other stakeholders. But for changes in corporate governance to influence the extent to which so-called triple bottom line issues are specifically reflected in company accounts, they would probably need to be accompanied by other regulation.

Elsewhere, nonaccounting reporting on environmental, health, and safety issues has been a legal requirement in several countries for some years—for instance, the TRI reporting requirements in the United States and the Integrated Pollution

---

[30]The U.S. acid rain (SO_2, NO_2) trading scheme is accounted for under FAS 71, *Accounting for the Effects of Certain Types of Regulation.*

[31]Currently, IAS 37 and IAS 20 apply to the recognition of emission rights, although the procedure is under review.

Prevention and Control Directive (IPPC) in Europe (European Union 1996).[32] When such schemes are introduced, analysts can incorporate into their models previously externalized costs, which might be seen as a leveling of the economic (as well as the environmental and social) playing field.

In short, when regulations are introduced, they are about connecting externalities to finance, and when it is successful, it could be said that the bottom line moves slightly closer to the triple bottom line. But it is not sufficient in the eyes of many of the firm's stakeholders if so-called triple bottom line issues are reported only when they become overtly financial. As a measure of how many firms report on triple bottom line issues, a U.K. report on environmental disclosure found that 89 percent of FTSE All-Share companies discuss their interaction with the environment in the annual reports, 24 percent make quantitative disclosures, and 11 percent make a link to financial performance (Trucost 2004).

The triple bottom line concept, illustrated in **Exhibit 4.1**, is based on the thinking that by focusing exclusively on the financial bottom line, traditional financial statements do not present the full picture of corporate performance. The triple bottom line approach is based on the construct that society is dependent on the economy and the economy, in turn, on the environment or "global ecosystem." In essence, the triple bottom line concept is about accounting for social externalities (see also Chapter 2) and, of course, about addressing stakeholder issues (see also Chapter 3). Although this concept may seem to be far removed from conventional accounting approaches, this extension should be seen as a natural evolution of the way company reports are used because companies have become a more dominant part of everyday life over the years.

Exhibit 4.1.   Triple Bottom Line

1	Social bottom line
2	Economic bottom line
3	Environmental bottom line

Source: Based on Elkington (1999, p. 73).

Even where environmental and social reporting is not mandatory, pressure from a wide range of stakeholders is, therefore, "making it almost implicitly essential to maintaining a license to operate" (ABI 2002, p. 1). One problem facing firms seeking to report is that the range of issues that could be reported in a triple bottom line context is potentially infinite, and it may not always be obvious what should be reported. Clearly, from a corporate point of view, whatever is closest to the firm's core strategy matters the most. For firms that consider the environmental and social

---

[32]See KPMG (2005, pp. 40–42) for a list of mandatory reporting requirements by country.

impacts of any corporate strategy as integral to that strategy, deciding what to report should, therefore, pose no problem. If social and environmental issues are not routinely considered as integral to corporate strategy, it may not be obvious what matters even to the firms themselves. The most recent version of the Carbon Disclosure Project contains some good examples among the corporate responses to survey questions, shown in **Exhibit 4.2**.

Exhibit 4.2.   Climate Change: Relevant or Not? Responses to Survey Questions

Industry	Relevant?	Not Relevant?
Food and drug retailing	"Could affect the procurement and quality of raw materials."	"Not relevant. . . . production of greenhouse gases is limited."
Pharmaceuticals	"Material risk."	"Not of highly significant relevance."
Broadcasting and cable TV	"Poses both commercial risks and opportunities to our business."	"Irrelevant to our industry."

Source: Based on Innovest Strategic Value Advisors (2005, p. 28).

Reporting Frameworks and Guidelines: Expert Groups

The need to establish some reporting ground rules is reflected in the existence of a number of reporting frameworks or guidelines developed by different stakeholder groups to articulate what is needed in company disclosures. These frameworks take several forms: voluntary guidelines produced by expert SRI industry bodies, such as the Global Reporting Initiative (GRI); voluntary guidelines and recommendations produced by international coalitions, such as the OECD, or by governments or government bodies, such as the EU or DEFRA; and principles set down by nongovernment organizations that, although not directly focusing on reporting, would be likely to influence what is reported in company accounts in such a way as to move them closer to the triple bottom line concept.

The GRI, described on the GRI website as a "multi-stakeholder process and independent institution whose mission is to develop and disseminate globally applicable Sustainability Reporting Guidelines," is for voluntary use by organizations for reporting on the economic, environmental, and social aspects of their activities, products, and services. The number of firms using it as a reference framework appears to be growing steadily. Although the social–economic–environmental hierarchy is reshuffled, see **Exhibit 4.3**, the GRI framework essentially embraces a version of the triple bottom line approach. The guidelines were first issued in 2000, updated in 2002, and now the third generation guidelines—the G3 or third generation—are expected in late 2006.

Exhibit 4.3. GRI's Sustainability Reporting Guidelines—Extracts

Triple Bottom Line Category	Category/Aspect
Economic	Direct economic impacts (e.g., customers, suppliers, employees, providers of capital).
Environmental	Environmental impacts (e.g., materials, energy, water, biodiversity, emissions, suppliers, products and services, compliance).
Social	Labor practices and decent work (e.g., employment, health and safety, training, diversity).
	Human rights (e.g., freedom of association, child labor, forced and compulsory labor, security practices).
	Society (e.g., community, political contributions, competition, and pricing).
	Product responsibility (e.g., customer health and safety, advertising).

Notes: The third generation project has the support and sponsorship of a number of firms: Alcan, BP, Ford Motor Company, General Motors, Microsoft Corporation, Royal Bank of Canada, and Shell. Governmental supporters include the EC and the Netherlands. See GRI website for a full breakdown of the guidelines.

Source: Based on information from the GRI website, listed in Appendix B.

Many of the GRI reporting categories may not be easily incorporated into conventional accounting frameworks, but they may be effective as internal operating or working guidelines. In another noteworthy development, GRI representatives are participating in the development of the forthcoming ISO 26000 Guidance Standard for Social Responsibility. The International Organization for Standardization (ISO) is an organization that focuses on management systems and operating practices and is well known for its environmental management standards series 14000. GRI's aims are to ensure that its Sustainability Reporting Guidelines can be used in conjunction with any management system that may emerge from the ISO process. In general, environmental accounting appears to be more developed as a management accounting approach than a reporting framework, with few guidelines available on the subject of reporting but with a substantial body of information on management accounting.[33] The net result should be that business-critical environmental or social impacts (almost inevitably) appear somewhere in the financial statements even if not specifically identified because "management accounting" implies business impact, which leads straight back to an earlier point: What is reported on in a triple bottom line sense should be what is most important to any firm's core business strategy. If it is already an integral part of the firm's management systems, then reporting on social, economic, and environmental impacts is unlikely to be a major step. Unsurprisingly, the approaches taken by other expert bodies—such as ABI (2001), AccountAbility (1999), and FORGE Group (2002)—in their respective guidelines and frameworks, comment on the need to integrate triple bottom line reporting with the core business.

[33] See, for example, Bennett, Rikhardsson, and Schaltegger (2003).

The Link between Reporting and Performance

Accounting, reporting, and disclosure are not just about describing a firm's financial, operating, environmental, or social performance but are about the shaping of the way firms compete in their core businesses. Just the fact that a firm is reporting to a broad range of stakeholders on such issues may change the way it operates more generally, and indeed, the appearance of information may also have an impact on the valuation of the firm's liabilities (debt, equity) in financial markets.

Operating changes may arise because having the firm's published information become available may rely on the firm's monitoring and control systems (perhaps changing the way they are used) or, alternatively, require that new monitoring and control systems be put in place. The ISO, for instance, audits and rates firms as compliant when their internal reporting and management systems have reached the required standard with respect to a wide number of issues, including some that fall specifically into the CSR area, namely, ISO 9000 (Quality), ISO 14000 (Environment), and ISO 20000 (Supply Chain).[34] Not all the information that influences the ranking is publicly available in the firm's financial statements, but if the management practices that have been adopted have an impact on the business, chances are that their influence will have an impact on what is reported, either directly or indirectly.

Reporting Frameworks: Governments

The U.K. 2002 white paper "Modernising Company Law" was followed in 2005 by the Accounting Standards Board (ASB) Reporting Standard 1 (RS 1), *Operating and Financial Review* (OFR), which was, until November 2005, expected to be mandatory for all U.K. quoted companies for financial years beginning on or after 1 April 2005. On 28 November 2005, in a speech by Chancellor Gordon Brown, the U.K. Treasury unexpectedly announced that the OFR would be scrapped.[35] The OFR was to be a narrative report intended to complement the firm's financial statements. Although addressed to shareholders (Summary Paragraph b and Paragraph 8), the information disclosed in the OFR was expected to be relevant to other stakeholders but was not intended to be "a replacement for other forms of reporting addressed to a wider stakeholder group." Paragraph 28 stated that the OFR was required to give shareholders enough information to assess the firm's strategies and

---

[34]The ISO describes itself as a global network that identifies what international standards are required by business, government, and society, relating to quality, ecology, safety, economy, reliability, compatibility, interoperability, efficiency, and effectiveness. It develops the relevant voluntary standards in partnership with the sectors that will put them to use. It also works on the basis of a consultative, multistakeholder process.

[35]The speech can be found online at www.hm-treasury.gov.uk/newsroom_and_speeches/press/2005/press_99_05.cfm.

their potential for success, and to the extent necessary to comply with Paragraph 8 on shareholders and other stakeholders, the firm would also have been required to disclose the following:

- environmental matters (including the impact of the business of the entity on the environment),
- the entity's employees,
- social and community issues,
- persons with whom the entity has contractual or other arrangements that are essential to the business of the entity,
- receipts from, and returns to, members of the entity in respect of shares held by them, and
- all other matters the directors consider to be relevant.

In this way, U.K. firms were, from 2005 onwards, expected to have to consider carefully the need to disclose CSR information, although precisely what was to be reported was not prescribed. Rather, the firm's commercial and business priorities were expected to determine the precise content. As noted in Chapter 2, everyone is waiting to see whether, after the surprise announcement of November 2005, firms continue to produce OFRs on a voluntary basis because doing so would be the best test of the suitability of the regulation.

Elsewhere, it is possible to identify a substantial amount of guideline material in the area of environmental issues. In the United States, the EPA has issued a wide range of guidelines and guidance. For instance, in 1995, the EPA published "An Introduction to Environmental Accounting as a Business Management Tool: Key Concepts and Terms," which discusses the spectrum of environmental costs—conventional, hidden, contingent, image/relational, and societal. The difference between private costs and societal costs is explored together with applications of environmental accounting to cost allocation, capital budgeting, and process/product design. In this, and later documents, the focus is (once again) on management and cost accounting—in other words, the internal perspective of the firm rather than the firm's external reports to shareholders and other stakeholders.[36] McDaniel, Gadkari, and Fiksel (2000) discussed the concept of the environmental EVA, hinting at an interesting direction that does not yet appear to have been pursued further.[37] In Europe, the European Commission recommended that companies in member states covered by the fourth and seventh Company Law Directives (Directives 78/660/EEC and 83/349/EEC, respectively) apply its guidelines on environmental reporting in the preparation of the annual and consolidated accounts and the annual report and consolidated annual report, take the appropriate measures to

---

[36]For a list of U.S. EPA environmental accounting documents, see www.epa.gov/oppt/acctg/sources.htm. See also the Environmental Management Accounting website, www.emawebsite.org; in particular, UN Division for Sustainable Development (2001).
[37]See also Ehrbar (1998) for an account of EVA.

promote the application of this recommendation, and notify the commission of the measures taken.[38] The main provisions of the recommendation are shown in **Exhibit 4.4**. Their significance in this context is that they are relatively rare in their setting out reporting principles (rather than management accounting principles).

Guidelines: Nongovernment Organizations and Other Coalitions

As would be expected, nongovernment organizations and other coalitions focus on guiding principles or, alternatively, compacts or conventions to which organizations

---

Exhibit 4.4. EU Guidelines on Environmental Reporting: Extracts

Recognition of environmental liabilities

1. An environmental liability is recognized when it is probable that an outflow of resources embodying economic benefits will result from the settlement of a present obligation of an environmental nature that arose from past events, and the amount at which the settlement will take place can be measured reliably. The nature of this obligation must be clearly defined and may be of two types—legal or constructive.

2. Past or current industry practice results in a constructive obligation for the enterprise only to the extent that management has no discretion to avoid action. It will only occur when the enterprise has accepted the responsibility to prevent, reduce, or repair environmental damage by a published specific statement or by an established pattern of past practice.

3. Environmental damage which may be related to the enterprise or may have been caused by the enterprise but for which there is no legal, contractual, or constructive obligation to rectify the damage's extent, does not qualify to be recognized as an environmental liability in the enterprise's annual accounts in accordance with paragraphs 1 and 2. This does not prejudice the application of the criteria set out in paragraph 5 for contingent environmental liabilities.

4. An environmental liability is recognized when a reliable estimate of the costs derived from the obligation can be made. If, at the date of the balance sheet, there is an obligation the nature of which is clearly defined and which is likely to give rise to an outflow of resources embodying economic benefits, but uncertain as to the amount or as to the date, then a provision should be recognized, provided that a reliable estimate can be made of the amount of the obligation. . . . In the rare circumstances where a reliable estimate of the costs is not possible, the liability should not be recognized. It should be regarded as a contingent liability.

Contingent environmental liabilities

5. A contingent liability should not be recognized in the balance sheet. If there is a possibility, which is less than probable, that the damage has to be rectified in the future but the obligation has yet to be confirmed by the occurrence of an uncertain event, a contingent liability should be disclosed in the notes to the annual accounts. If it is a remote possibility that the enterprise will have to incur an environmental expenditure or such expenditure will not be material, disclosure of such contingent liability is not required.

Source: Based on European Commission (2001, p. 37).

---

[38]See European Commission (2001). See also the "White Paper on Environmental Liability," Brussels (9 February 2000): http://europa.eu.int/comm/environment/liability/white_paper.htm.

 ©2006, The Research Foundation of CFA Institute

can commit.[39] The focus is mainly on the way firms conduct business as opposed to what should be reported, or how; nevertheless, some of these guidelines refer directly to the need for good communication. In addition, some rating agencies monitor compliance with these guidelines (see Chapter 1), which makes it more likely that firms will report on them. In recent years, a number of firms have signed up to codes of conduct, such as the Ceres Principles, the UN Global Compact, the Sullivan Principles—listed in Appendix A—or the Equator Principles.[40] The Ceres Principles are of note in making disclosure an important part of the undertaking, whereas the Sullivan Principles refer to internal reporting structures. According to the Ceres website:

> By endorsing the Ceres Principles, companies not only formalize their dedication to environmental awareness and accountability, but also actively commit to an ongoing process of continuous improvement, dialogue and comprehensive, systematic public reporting.

The Sullivan Principles, as put forth by the Sullivan Foundation, ask companies to agree to the following:

> As a company which endorses the Global Sullivan Principles we will undertake to respect the law, and as a responsible member of society to apply these Principles with integrity consistent with the legitimate role of business. We will develop and implement company policies, procedures, training and internal reporting structures to ensure commitment to these Principles throughout our organization.

Elsewhere, the UN Global Compact does not make a direct link to disclosure; however, later work in this context is of note.[41] For instance, a collaborative work involving a number of financial institutions signaled the importance of environmental, social, and governance factors for valuation in a report entitled "Who Cares Wins: Connecting Financial Markets to a Changing World" (UN Global Compact 2004).

Of course, just as stakeholders outside the firm can influence what is disclosed, disclosure has an influence on stakeholders outside the firm, which means the way information is presented can be important. Financial statements are, as noted earlier, sometimes focused on specific stakeholders, such as lenders or tax bodies. An interesting body of literature exists on the subject of alleged accruals manipulation by firms to influence regulatory bodies outside the firm (by apparently giving the impression of lower profitability than is actually the case) when regulatory

---

[39]For example, see OECD (2000).

[40]For a full list of the principles and the firms that have signed up, see the respective websites, listed in Appendix B.

[41]See also the Universal Declaration of Human Rights, the International Labor Organization's Declaration on Fundamental Principles and Rights at Work, the Rio Declaration on Environment and Development, and the United Nations Convention Against Corruption. The UN Global Compact's Ten Principles are derived from these declarations.

investigations are under way.[42] An article by Patten and Trompeter (2003) extends this analysis to environmental disclosures in the context of earnings management in response to a regulatory threat. This is a salutary reminder that information can be manipulated: Just as with any other form of financial reporting, it is a question of reader beware.

Environmental, Social, and Governance Issues in Conventional Accounting Frameworks

To some extent, conventional reporting frameworks have required the inclusion of some environmental and social issues, and to a certain degree, a framework exists to take them into account. For instance, some International Accounting Standards (IAS) are widely regarded as relevant to environmental issues—namely IAS 36 on impairment of assets; IAS 37 on provisions, contingent liabilities, and contingent assets; and IAS 38 on intangible assets. As noted in Chapter 2, IAS 37 states that liabilities that are uncertain in terms of amount or timing should be recognized only when an entity "has a present obligation (legal or constructive) as a result of a past event; it is probable that an outflow of resources embodying economic benefits will be required to settle the obligation; a reliable estimate can be made of the obligation." Contingent liabilities can be disclosed (if not remote) but should not be recognized. Elsewhere, the new version of IAS 38 states that an intangible asset must be identifiable, where identifiable is defined as separability ("capable of being divided from the entity and sold or in some other way exchanged; and must arise from contractual or other legal rights"[43]). The EU Guidelines on Environmental Reporting describe in more detail how accounting principles might be applied to environmental issues. More generally, conventional accounting standards exist to cover certain direct, quantifiable costs that fall into the "social" category, such as wages and salaries and other compensation. Similarly, when environmental costs become identifiable, quantifiable, and likely to crystallize, they fall under some of the accounting guidelines mentioned previously, demonstrated in **Exhibit 4.5** by linking the GRI Guidelines to International Accounting Standards.

Often, however, CSR issues are difficult to value, uncertain in terms of timing and amount, and not separable, and thus they do not classify for separate disclosure in financial statements. In practice, conventional accounting guidelines mean that evaluating "soft" issues—such as value created by successful recruitment or training and development, successful stress management programs, free health care treatment in the presence of HIV/AIDS, or successful diversity policies—should be the preserve of the analyst rather than the accountant. Of course, the indirect benefits

---

[42]See, for example, Cahan (1992) and Dechow, Sloan, and Sweeney (1996). See also Dechow and Schrand (2004).

[43]IAS 38, IN6, p. 1566.

 ©2006, The Research Foundation of CFA Institute

Exhibit 4.5. GRI: How It Links to a Conventional Accounting Approach

GRI Category	GRI Aspects	Conventional Accounting Coverage	Relevance to Finance or Business
Direct economic impacts	Customers; suppliers; employees; providers of capital; public sector.	IAS 19: *Employee Benefits.* Short-term benefits (wages, leave, profit sharing, nonmonetary benefits such as medical care, free or subsidized goods or services); postemployment benefits (pensions); other long-term benefits; termination benefits. IAS 32: *Financial Instruments: Disclosure and Presentation* IAS 33: *Earnings per Share* IAS 34: *Interim Financial Reporting* IAS 38: *Intangible Assets*	Costs, risk, value creation, inputs to valuation.
Environmental	Materials; energy; water; biodiversity; emissions effluents and waste; suppliers; products and services; compliance; transport.	IAS 36: *Impairment of Assets* IAS 37: *Provisions, Contingent Liabilities and Contingent Assets* IAS 38: *Intangible Assets* IAS 39: *Financial Instruments: Recognition and Measurement* (includes financial assets and liabilities held for trading) IAS 41: *Agriculture* IAS 20: *Accounting for Government Grants*	Operating costs. Risk profile. Access to capital. Shareholder value.
Labor practices and decent work	Employment, labor/management relations; health and safety; training and education; diversity and opportunity.	IAS 19: *Employee Benefits* IAS 37: *Provisions, Contingent Liabilities and Contingent Assets* IAS 38: *Intangible Assets*	Revenue. Productivity. Brand value. Human capital. Intellectual capital/intellectual property.
Human rights	Strategy and management; nondiscrimination; freedom of association and collective bargaining; child labor; forced and compulsory labor; disciplinary practices; security practices; indigenous rights.	IAS 19: *Employee Benefits* IAS 37: *Provisions, Contingent Liabilities and Contingent Assets* IAS 20: *Accounting for Government Grants and Disclosure of Government Assistance*	Operational risk. Revenue. Brand value.
Society	Community; bribery and corruption; political contributions; competition and pricing.	IAS 20: *Accounting for Government Grants and Disclosure of Government Assistance* IAS 24: *Related Party Disclosures*	Brand value. Operational risk.
Product responsibility	Customer health and safety; products and services; advertising; respect for privacy.	IAS 37: *Provisions, Contingent Liabilities and Contingent Assets* IAS 38: *Intangible Assets*	Brand value.

Note: This refers to the "G2" version of the GRI. G3 Guidelines are in draft, to be released in October 2006.

Source: Based on information from the GRI and IASB.

of getting such policies right (or the indirect costs of not doing so) should eventually appear in financial statements insofar as such success or failure affects the firm's core business and, therefore, its financial performance. But this benefit may accrue some time after it is relevant to the firm's economic value.

Overall, such reporting frameworks as the OFR and the GRI can be viewed as means of dealing with the grey area between hard items in financial statements and value created by the business in activities that might be classified as environmental, social, governance, or ethical. Ideally, reports and disclosures that go beyond accounting rules should be designed to give shareholders enough information to assess the firm's strategies and their potential for success.[44]

In general, the SRI or CSR reporting frameworks are at a relatively early stage of development compared with established reporting standards (with perhaps one notable exception—the RS 1 described previously, developed by the U.K. Accounting Standards Board). For analysts attempting to assess the added value generated by firms over time or relative to their peer group, no well-defined, widely used comparators exist. In Chapter 5, some evidence suggests that environmental, social, and governance performance indicators may be useful markers for value creation. Without doubt, more and more firms are reporting on CSR issues.[45] Some of the research service providers and index providers—ISS, GMI, Innovest, EIRIS, and Trucost, to name a few—have built up quite comprehensive databases. A recent report on eco-efficiency by Derwall, Guenster, Bauer, and Koedijk (2005) draws on such data in an effective manner to demonstrate an association between environmental performance and financial performance. To replicate such a study for a wider range of relevant issues (beyond environmental issues) and to do so on a global basis meets considerable practical problems and, therefore, still appears to be some way off.[46] For instance, even when most of the firms in a relevant cohort report on specific performance indicators, such as energy use, CO_2 emissions, or water usage, there is no widely accepted reporting methodology, which means that, in practice, comparing firms with their peers is often impossible. Reporting practices may be changing gradually as financial statements evolve to become focused on a broader range of stakeholders; nevertheless, there seems to be some way to go before Black's (1980) ideal may be reached.

The critical point to drop out of this chapter is that the triple bottom line concept is influencing the content and structure of financial statements, which is something no investor can afford to ignore. In this regard, the discipline of SRI brings a valuable perspective to the table for investment decision makers.

---

[44]See the previous discussion of OFR.

[45]See Lyndenberg (2005) for an overview of trends in reporting.

[46]For example, Gompers, Ishii, and Metrick (2001) found an association between the quality of corporate governance and financial performance for U.S. firms. Replicating this study beyond the United States would be extremely difficult owing to a lack of raw data.

                    ©2006, The Research Foundation of CFA Institute

5. Literature Survey: Analytical Approaches Applied to SRI

Both academic and practitioner literature have attempted to link social responsibility and financial performance from several perspectives, ranging from the impact on corporate profitability, to the impact on asset values (share price performance and valuation), to the impact on the performance of managed portfolios and SRI indices. The aim of this chapter is, above all, to draw out important threads in the literature rather than to be fully comprehensive. For those interested in exploring further, a good place to begin is the annotated bibliography maintained by Lloyd Kurtz.[47] Alternatively, Margolis and Walsh (2001) summarized 95 empirical studies.

Impact of Social Responsibility on Corporate Performance: Corporate Perspective

Contrasting views exist with respect to social performance and its likely effect on firms. On one side is the view that the costs of adhering to high environmental and social standards will translate to higher operating costs, translating, in turn, to a competitive disadvantage and lower profitability. The other side is the view that strong social policies confer a competitive advantage by one or more of several means: stimulating technology innovations, improving the efficiency of resource use thereby cutting costs, strengthening a firm's reputation and brand, or reducing operational risk. It is quite likely that both negative and positive effects can be observed and, therefore, that both views are right, depending on the context. In particular, it is likely that the structure of the relevant market will determine the interplay between social costs and competition. Bakan (2004) described the corporation as the efficient externalizer. Firms, however, may also have an incentive to internalize costs if by doing so they can compete more effectively against their peers. When competition effects are likely to prevail against firms following good environmental and social practice, then a regulatory approach (whether industry or government) may be required to resolve the resulting problem of cost externalization unless firms themselves are able to establish

---

[47]Found online at www.sristudies.org.

voluntary norms individually or as a group. When such a situation arises, it should not necessarily be seen as a negative for company profitability:

> Some localities (or user industries) will lead in terms of the stringency of product standards, pollution limits, noise guidelines, and the like. Tough regulatory standards are not a hindrance but an opportunity to move early to upgrade products and processes. (Porter 1998, pp. 585–586)

Currently, an interesting phenomenon may be occurring in this context: Firms that have historically pursued energy efficiency where others have not (for instance, Japanese auto manufacturers) may be gaining a comparative advantage in their sector. This advantage is the result of a combination of regulation (taxation on fuel costs in certain countries) and market forces (higher oil prices). Such an advantage may be only temporary because others in the industry can catch up. But if the technology lead is used to cement market share, a comparative advantage can become a competitive advantage.[48]

Several possible approaches can be used to look at the impact of environmental and social performance on corporate performance, as follows. From the corporate perspective of production management, the impact of investments in environmental or social "factors of production" might be observable through their effect on productive efficiency. Much of the research in this area has focused on environmental performance rather than on social issues, such as human capital management, probably because the effects of such investments are more difficult to identify or quantify. From an accounting perspective [and thinking in terms of the DuPont return on equity (ROE) decomposition], the impacts of social responsibility on corporate performance might be expected to be observable in terms of effect on sales growth (or market share), on efficiency (asset turnover), on profit margins (through cost savings, or price effects), or on measures of return—such as return on equity (ROE) or return on assets (ROA).[49] In fact, much of the work that has been undertaken in the area of SRI, insofar as it relates to an accounting profit perspective, has focused on the impact of CSR performance on a small number of measures of profitability or return (mainly ROE and sometimes ROA and profit margins). Very little work seems to exist that focuses on efficiency in the narrow sense of asset turnover, but it does appear as a metric in a small number of studies. For instance, Margolis and Walsh (2001) summarize Rockness, Schlachter, and Rockness (1986) who list asset turnover along with ROE, ROA, return on sales, and other measures of financial performance. Alternatively, the effects of CSR issues may be observed as changes in the calculated value of the firm, namely, on the net present value of enterprise cash flows, and some important work has begun to focus on this area in

---

[48]With thanks to Paul Donovan for this comment.
[49]Note that accounting effects (mainly timing effects) may mask the real impact of firm CSR strategies on (apparent) firm performance if accounting data are the main focus of research.

    ©2006, The Research Foundation of CFA Institute

recent years. The following sections on corporate performance consider literature in the following areas, in turn: productive efficiency, profit margins, profitability, risk, and calculated firm value.

Productive Efficiency. The substantial body of literature on environmental performance and productive efficiency is explored only briefly here. The most important work for the purposes of this monograph is the Porter hypothesis.[50] The Porter hypothesis argues that environmental regulation not only improves environmental conditions but also can increase production efficiency and hence the competitiveness of manufacturers. The idea that firms could invest in environmental efficiency and also gain at the level of operating efficiency is appealing; however, the research evidence is mixed. Marklund (2003), for instance, found no support for the Porter hypothesis. Esty and Porter (1998, p. 41) also noted that firms can apply industrial ecology without necessarily suffering increased costs, but they stated that it will depend on the regulatory framework in place. Khanna and Kumar (2005), however, found the comprehensiveness of an environmental management system (EMS) to have a significant effect on the environmental efficiency of firms in terms of a lower opportunity cost of reducing pollution.

Perhaps the key implication of the Porter hypothesis is that with the right regulatory structure in place, it may be possible to align competition effects so that firms competing to be environmentally efficient are also competing to be efficient in a broader sense. This hypothesis appears to be supported by research in the area of operations management (OM), which initially focused on the avenue of total quality management (TQM) but also later on supply-chain management (SCM).[51] If such initiatives are successful, better operating efficiency (than the competition) would be expected to translate to higher profitability, all other things being equal.

Relatedly, Dowell, Hart, and Yeung (2000) observed that firms applying higher home-base environmental standards elsewhere, rather than accepting locally prevailing lower standards in other geographical locations, may potentially find themselves facing a higher cost curve than competitors in the new environment. Therefore, the obvious incentive is to lower environmental performance standards. They concluded, however, that firms that default to the lower environmental standards, falling into line with local practices, may find doing so to be counterproductive to long-term profit performance. The commentary of Konar and Cohen (2000) (see also Chapter 3) is also supportive of the view that environmental efficiency may translate to a stronger overall competitive performance under the right conditions.

---

[50] See Porter (1998); see also Porter and Van der Linde (1995a) and (1995b).

[51] For a summary of trends in the literature on SCM, see Corbett and Klassen (2006).

Profit Margins. Profit margins may be affected by cost cutting, price effects, or indeed, by accounting effects. Some measures taken to mitigate corporate social factors can bring cost improvements in their wake (such as a reduction in fossil fuel use to reduce CO_2 emissions, which also cuts fuel costs for the firm). Firms whose products have a high price elasticity of demand may be unable to pass on any increased costs associated with corporate social responsibility policies. Conversely, firms specializing in highly discretionary goods may find it relatively easy to hold on to any cost improvements or to pass on any increased costs to the customer. A further possibility is that strong CSR policies may enhance brand value, which may be positive rather than negative for profit margins if it translates to higher product prices.

In practice, such price effects are extremely difficult to identify or quantify, and so, unsurprisingly, little research appears to have been conducted in this area. This situation, however, may change: The appearance of products specifically labeled environmentally friendly, such as the ENERGY STAR series in the United States and Japan, may at some stage deliver enough data to allow an empirical assessment of the impact of environmental policies on brand value. Alternatively, the arrival on the scene of "clean vehicles" in the auto sector is an empirical test, in action, of the consumer's willingness to pay to be environmentally responsible.

In general, empirical research suggests that investments in environmental and social performance seem to be helpful for profit margins; however, the authors of this research often also qualify their results on the basis that execution will affect the results. Hart and Ahuja (1996) presented evidence indicating that efforts to prevent pollution and reduce emissions are positively associated with return on sales in the following year (p. 35). Austin et al. (2003) looked at the potential impact on automakers of complying with CO_2 emission regulation and concluded that one implication of their analysis is the potential for lower EBIT (earnings before interest and taxes) margins for the industry as a whole. They noted, however, that this may not be the whole story:

> Though vehicle pricing is currently very competitive, if the industry as a whole is facing pressure to lower carbon intensity, it is likely that average vehicle prices will rise as OEMs try to recoup costs. Moreover, over a 10-year period, there is ample scope for OEMs to raise vehicle prices: since 1970, the average amount that US consumers have been willing to spend on a new vehicle has increased by $229 each year. (p. 40)

More generally, Waddock and Graves (1997) looked at the relationship between profit margins and an index of corporate social performance constructed from KLD rankings of firms on the basis of community relations, employee relations, the environment, product characteristics, treatment of women and minorities, military contracting, participation in nuclear power, and involvement in South Africa (which was relevant during the time period of analysis).[52] A positive relationship was found between CSR performance and profit margin.

---

[52]Note that the model is adjusted for industry, firm size, and firm capital structure.

Return on Assets/Return on Equity. The Waddock and Graves (1997) work also found a positive relationship between their CSR index and ROA and ROE. Hart and Ahuja (1996) examined the relationship between emissions reduction and profitability (defined as ROA and ROE) for a sample of S&P 500 Index firms and found that efforts to prevent pollution and reduce emissions "drop to the bottom line within one to two years of initiation and that those firms with the highest emission levels stand the most to gain" (p. 30).

Cohen, Fenn, and Konar (1997) created two baskets of firms: firms having low and high scores, respectively, on nine measures of environmental risk. Their results suggest a positive association between two measures of accounting return (ROA and ROE) and an investment in pollution prevention. They pointed out, however, that it is not certain which way causality runs: Firms may be able to invest in pollution prevention because strong financial performance means they can afford to do so, or strong financial performance may be the result of investment in pollution control.

Russo and Fouts (1997) controlled for a number of industry factors, including industry concentration, industry growth rate, firm growth rate, firm size, capital intensity, and advertising intensity. They found that the environmental rating as defined by Franklin Research and Development Corporation is associated with a higher ROA. Mahoney and Roberts (2002), using four years of panel data for a sample of Canadian firms, found a significant and positive relationship between a firm's environmental performance and its financial performance.

Nehrt (1996) examined the relationship between timing and intensity of investment in pollution prevention and growth in profits within a sample of 50 pulp and paper companies. These results indicate a positive relationship between early movers in pollution prevention and profit growth. But: "There is also evidence that more intense investment patterns, when not tempered by sufficient time to absorb the investments, may lead to lower profit growth" (Nehrt 1996, p. 535). The most recent work in this area at the time of writing, Guenster, Derwall, and Bauer (2005), found that, although environmental leaders do not appear to outperform a control group of firms, return on assets of environmental "laggards" shows significant underperformance.

The striking point about research in this area is how much research seems to be in support of the positive link between environmental performance and profitability—see also Murphy (2002) for a review of the literature finding a similarly positive bias—and how little making the reverse case, which may perhaps be explained by research publication bias (the possibility that positive findings are more likely to be published). But because environmental performance is likely to be directly tied to the efficient use of resources and environmental regulation has progressively tightened in recent decades, the positive bias of the published research identified in this survey does not seem unreasonable over the specific time period to which the relevant data relate. As noted previously, when it is profitable to do so, firms have an incentive to internalize their environmental impact without further ado, and the prevailing regulatory framework is likely to determine when that is (or is not) the case.

Risk. The impact of CSR policies on risk may be direct, involving, for example, greater or lesser flexibility with respect to the management of the balance sheet. Or, it may be indirect, affecting the firm through the cost at which it may raise funds in the market. Far less work exists on the impact of CSR performance on risk than on profitability or return. Margolis and Walsh (2001) identified the use of the debt-to-equity ratio as a measure of financial performance in just six studies and the current ratio in four. What research does exist suggests that strong CSR policies may at times reduce risk. Pava and Krausz (1996) looked at several accounting risk measures (debt-to-equity, interest cover, liquidity ratios) and found no impact. The work of Feldman, Soyka, and Ameer (1997) suggests that improved environmental performance might lead to a reduction in the perceived risk of a firm, with an accompanying increase in a firm's stock price.

Garber and Hammitt (1998) found that the equity betas of 73 large U.S.-listed chemical companies appear to vary with Superfund liabilities between 1976 and 1992. Elsewhere, Navarro (1988) reviewed corporate-giving data for 249 U.S. firms for 1978, 1981, and 1983 and found that contributions are negatively related to firm debt and positively related to firm dividends. This article is of interest in this context because this conclusion raises the question of direction of causality. Is it, simply, the case that firms having a lower financial risk profile (as represented in lower gearing and more available cash for the payment of dividends) are better able to afford corporate giving? Or, conversely, is it the case that firms having a proclivity to corporate giving are (as a result of the accompanying management mindset) lower risk? This question is impossible to answer, but of course, in a sense, the direction of causality does not matter. If strong environmental and social performance (be it in the form of strong environmental performance or an appropriate corporate-giving program) are a marker for lower risk more generally, that information should be considered useful to all investors and analysts, whatever their investment style.

Impact of CSR on Calculated Firm Value (Present Value of Future Cash Flows). The use of accounting profit to diagnose the effects of CSR policies has its limitations, as discussed in Chapter 2. Discounted cash flow (DCF) models have the advantage of capturing a more complete picture of firm performance. Their disadvantage is that they require input parameters that simply cannot be observed. The cost of capital, and cash flows in the long term, are unknowns. DCF work has the benefit that it corrects for the timing issues encountered in accounting measures of performance. Net–net results, however, may be harder to interpret and may always be open to question.

Nevertheless, as some of the work that has been done shows, DCF exercises can be useful in giving an idea of the likely scale of the impact of CSR effects. Repetto and Austin (2000), for example, used a combination of DCF and scenario analysis to estimate the economic impact of environmental risks (in the form of future regulation) to 13 major U.S. pulp and paper companies. Their work showed that for their sample of 13 firms, the net impact of environmental exposure ranged from +2.9 percent to −10.8 percent of the firms' calculated market value (p. 47, Table 4). Elsewhere, Austin and Sauer (2002) applied similar methodology to examine the potential impact of climate policies and restricted access to reserves on global oil and gas companies. For several different scenarios—ranging from adoption of the Kyoto Protocol to no action—various climate policies could create "most likely" financial impacts for companies, ranging from a 5 percent loss in shareholder value to a slight gain (p. 2). Under some negative scenarios, calculated shareholder value could be affected by larger amounts for some companies. Austin et al. (2003) analyzed the impact of compliance with global carbon dioxide emission standards on global auto makers by calculating the effect of compliance in terms of percentage changes from business-as-usual discounted EBIT over the 2003–15 time frame.

Of course, the best guide of the impact of CSR effects on the value of the firm is likely to be found in the market, which is the subject of the next section.

Impact of Social Responsibility on Asset Prices

Empirical work on the impact of CSR effects on asset prices tends to take one of four forms: (1) a look at share price effects in response to specific events, (2) an analysis of valuation effects in response to specific attributes (usually relating to environmental performance) in cross-sections of firms, (3) an examination of the performance of existing SRI portfolios, and (4) the creation of synthetic portfolios or baskets of stocks to analyze the performance. This section is directly relevant to the discussion in Chapter 1, in which beliefs relating to financial markets were suggested for each SRI portfolio type. Key beliefs are summarized in **Exhibit 5.1**.

Exhibit 5.1 makes it clear that the questions that are relevant to all portfolio managers also apply in an SRI context. The risk–return profile of portfolios run on the basis of each category in Exhibit 5.1 is contingent on questions of market efficiency and manager skill as much as the way in which SRI-related beliefs are incorporated. Any attempt to evaluate the impact of social responsibility on asset price performance encounters exactly the same problems as any other empirical exercise in the field of finance. To evaluate empirically the hypothesis that social responsibility affects share prices for better or worse is a simultaneous test of the model used—the same problem faced by anyone testing the efficient market hypothesis (EMH).

Exhibit 5.1. SRI Approaches and Beliefs about Efficient Markets and Fund Manager Skill

SRI Approach	Efficient Market Hypothesis (EMH) Accepted?	Fund Manager Skill Accepted?
Exclusion	Irrelevant: The aim is to maximize wealth within values-based constraints.	Not necessarily relevant where stock selection is concerned. Information search relating to values-based constraints is the key point.
Best in Class	Weak form EMH may be valid, but semi-strong form may not hold.	Yes. Best-in-class SRI investors look to identify return relating to CSR-related information.
Engagement	Weak form and semi-strong form may be valid, but strong form not.	Yes. Fund manager skill lies in identifying companies in which a change of operating practice may increase shareholder value.
Advocacy/ Activism	Depends on the precise investment aim: To address the free-rider problem or to change firms with a view to adding to shareholder value.	Depends on the precise aim. Advocacy can be conducted in the context of an otherwise passive or active portfolio, or in the context of an exclusion portfolio.

Share Price Performance. Many event studies in the area of SRI, particularly in the area of environmental information disclosures, find a relationship between information disclosures and share price performance. Most of these studies are, essentially, supportive of the semi-strong form of the EMH, which states that all public information is reflected in asset prices: Because the impact of significant CSR-related news on share prices is instantaneous, it is unlikely to be possible to exploit it to earn abnormal risk-adjusted returns. Some of these studies, however, suggest that there may be potential anomalies to exploit.

In the long list of event studies in this area, some found no impact of social issues on share price performance. Cohen, Fenn, and Konar (1997), for instance, found no statistical difference in the risk-adjusted total return of "low polluters" and "high polluters" based on a ranking of firms by industry. But many do. Instantaneous adjustment to news has been observed in many instances. Hamilton (1995) observed statistically significant abnormal negative returns in response to the EPA Toxics Release Inventory (TRI). Klassen and McLaughlin (1996) made use of the event-study approach to find a positive association between first-time environmental award announcements and financial performance (cumulative abnormal returns) and a negative impact of environmental crises on financial performance.

Govindaraj, Jaggi, and Lin (2004) examined a product-recall case and found substantial initial losses in the market value of the relevant firms. Also using the standard event-study approach, Filbeck and Gorman (2004) found that the announcement of an environmental award tends to produce consistent positive abnormal returns. Dasgupta, Laplante, and Mamingi (1997) assessed whether capital markets in Argentina, Chile, Mexico, and the Philippines react to the announcement of firm-specific environmental news. They found that capital markets react positively

©2006, The Research Foundation of CFA Institute

(increase in firms' market value) to the announcement of rewards and explicit recognition of superior environmental performance; they also found that capital markets react negatively (decrease in firms' value) to citizens' complaints.

So far, such studies are similar to other studies in the field of finance: The authors found that it is possible to identify events that appear to have affected asset prices, thereby indicating that CSR issues have financial impact. The next question is, of course, whether any of these effects take time to be reflected in asset prices—in short, whether the field of SRI can identify investable anomalies.[53]

Some of the empirical work, indeed, appears to identify apparent anomalies, thus potentially challenging the semi-strong version of the EMH. Hamilton (1995, p. 109) found significantly negative abnormal returns not only on the day of the announcement but also over a five-day window following the announcement. (The immediate fall in the share price on the announcement is consistent with the semi-strong version of the EMH, but the continuing drift in the share prices after the event may not be.) Govindaraj et al. (2004), in their study on product recall, found not only that the initial loss in the market value of the relevant firms was far in excess of direct costs associated with recall but also that firms later recovered their market value.

Cohen, Fenn, and Konar (1997) analyzed share price reactions to oil spills and found what appears to be a delayed reaction to the event in question (Section IV (d) of the paper). On a slightly different note, White's (1996) work on the Exxon Valdez looked at the impact of the oil spill on seemingly unrelated firms. He found that firms with a positive reputation for environmental responsibility earned superior risk-adjusted returns vis-à-vis their counterparts (p. 11). Guenster et al. (2005) found that the market appears to incorporate environmental information with a drift.

Overall, several event studies in the area of CSR suggest that some environmental performance indicators may be significant "markers," in the sense that it may at times be possible to use such markers to construct portfolios of stocks that outperform the market (see also the section below on best-in-class portfolio performance in which portfolios are constructed on the basis of such risk markers).

Impacts on Valuation. Studies attempting to identify an association (or lack thereof) between valuation metrics and measures of corporate social responsibility have a range of possibilities to choose from—the price-to-earnings ratio (P/E), enterprise value (EV) multiples (such as EV/EBIT), or the q ratio, defined as the market value of the enterprise divided by the replacement cost of its assets.[54] Preferred metrics in the context of recent empirical work in the field of SRI appear to be Tobin's q, the price-to-book ratio, and P/E.[55]

---

[53]For work in a non-SRI context that finds instantaneous adjustment, see Keown and Pinkerton (1981). For work that finds share price adjustment with a time lag, see also the well-known standard unexpected earnings (SUE) study, briefly described in Shleifer (2000).

[54]The advantages and disadvantages of Tobin's q as a measure of firm value are well known. See Lindenberg and Ross (1981).

[55]See, for example, studies tabulated by Margolis and Walsh (2001, pp. 18–19).

Dowell et al. (2000) analyzed the global environmental standards of a sample of U.S.-based multinational enterprises (MNEs) in relationship to their stock market performance and found that firms adopting a single stringent global environmental standard have much higher market values, as measured by Tobin's q, than firms defaulting to less stringent, or poorly enforced, host country standards. (The authors noted that Tobin's q is known to be related to capital structure, such intangibles as R&D and advertising expenditures, and multinationality and thus adjusted for these factors in their model.) Guenster et al. (2005) found evidence of a positive but nonlinear relationship between corporate eco-efficiency and the firm's Tobin's q. Khanna, Kumar, and Anton (2004) found that environmental liability costs and the negative reputational effects of significant toxic releases negatively affect a firm's profitability as defined by Tobin's q (viewed as a risk-adjusted prevent value of future profits). Konar and Cohen (2001) found weak environmental performance to be negatively correlated with the intangible asset value of firms, which is estimated as a component of Tobin's q. King and Lenox (2001) analyzed the relationship between a firm's toxic emissions and, again, Tobin's q. They found evidence of some association between lower levels of toxic emissions and a higher valuation; however:

> Much of the variance in our study is attributed to firm-level differences. Better understanding of these differences might provide a richer understanding of profitable environmental improvement. It may be that it pays to reduce pollution by certain means and not others. Alternatively, it may be that only firms with certain attributes can profitably reduce their pollution. (p. 113)

This observation serves as a reminder that if environmental or social performance is used as a marker of potentially superior performance, such information is likely to be best used in combination with other relevant information.

Impact of SRI on Portfolio Performance: Investment Styles

Some widely held, and quite contradictory, beliefs relate to SRI and portfolio performance in general. Some believe that the application of SRI strategies does not make any difference, at least in the short run, to portfolio returns or portfolio risk. Some believe that the application of an SRI constraint will manifest itself as a cost in risk-adjusted performance terms. Others believe that some SRI approaches may result in superior risk-adjusted performance either because firms that perform well in environmental and social terms also perform well as companies or because the risk controls implicit in some SRI screens reduce overall portfolio risk. **Exhibit 5.2** provides a summary of these views.

Exhibit 5.2. Efficient Markets, Manager Skill, and Benchmarks

SRI Approach	Efficient Market Hypothesis (EMH) Accepted?	Fund Manager Skill Accepted?	Benchmark Risk Considerations
Exclusion	Irrelevant: The aim is to maximize wealth within values-based constraints.	Fund manager may be able to make substitution trades that reduce benchmark-relative risk even if the information search relating to values-based constraints is the key point.	With pure exclusion portfolios, some divergence is expected.
Best in class	Weak form EMH may be valid, but semi-strong form may not hold.	Yes. Best-in-class SRI investors look to identify return relating to CSR performance.	Best-in-class investors tend to use conventional benchmarks. See left.
Engagement	Weak form and semi-strong form may be valid, but strong form not.	Yes. Fund manager skill lies in identifying companies in which a change of operating practice may increase shareholder value.	At the extreme, concentrated engagement portfolios may view absolute risk as more important than benchmark risk.
Advocacy/ Activism	Depends on the precise investment aim: To address the free-rider problem or to change firms with a view to adding to shareholder value.	Depends on the investment aim. Advocacy can be conducted in the context of an otherwise passive or active portfolio, or in the context of an exclusion portfolio.	Depends on the overall investment aim. See left.

Note: See also Exhibit 1.2.

To put such beliefs in context, it should be noted that, if SRI "factors" are already reflected in asset prices, then SRI strategies should be no more, nor less, profitable than any other active portfolio management strategy, on average. Some empirical work seems to support this hypothesis. On average, biasing portfolios toward "socially responsible" firms is likely to make little significant difference, whether positive or negative. But as with any active portfolio management style, to focus on the average may be to miss the point. Earlier sections suggested that, in specific situations, environmental or social corporate performance markers may be economically or financially significant. If it is, indeed, possible to identify such anomalies, then it may be possible for portfolios constructed on the basis of environmental or social criteria to outperform in risk-adjusted terms. Ultimately, of course, testing this hypothesis is not possible with any certainty. As noted earlier, any empirical work on this question is a simultaneous test of the model and the performance hypothesis.

The impact of socially responsible investment on portfolio performance has been assessed on the basis of a wide range of methodologies and models, incorporating advances in the theory of finance with the passage of time. The current state of the art in terms of approach is to adjust for the following factors in models: market risk and sector effects, size effects (Reinganum 1981; Banz 1981), style effects (growth versus value) (Fama and French 1993), and momentum effects (Carhart 1997). (See Chapter 6 for a review of finance theory as it relates to SRI.)

Whether the risk-adjusted expected returns of socially responsible portfolios are significantly different from the risk-adjusted expected returns of other styles of portfolio will also depend on the specific type of SRI portfolio. As discussed in Chapter 1, four approaches exist to social responsibility at the level of the investment portfolio, depending on the requirements of the ultimate decision maker in the chain: exclusion or screening of specific industries or companies on the basis of social criteria, ranking companies within industries to identify the best in class in terms of corporate social responsibility, engagement, and activism. These four investment styles are likely to have quite different consequences for the performance and risk profile of portfolios. It is extremely important in assessing the merits of SRI funds, in general, to be aware of the very different profiles of the investment approaches used. One of the problems faced by SRI, as a concept, is that this point is not often clearly articulated when the performance of SRI funds, in general, is discussed.

Exhibit 5.3 considers what evaluation framework may be relevant when assessing the performance of SRI funds. In short, conventional risk models may be adequate for the assessment of best-in-class portfolios. Some firms regard environmental and social performance as a basis on which they compete with other firms, and therefore, it is inseparable from the running of the business, in general. On this basis, even if it may be reasonable to suspect that pure exclusion portfolios can suffer diversification costs in the short run, there is no reason why best-in-class portfolios should have a significantly different risk profile from the average *actively managed* fund. Engagement portfolios may entail lower diversification because engagement may presuppose larger positions for engagement to take effect, which can be expected to translate to higher benchmark-relative risk in the short run.

Overall, any study that is based on data relating to different fund types (as described in Exhibit 5.3) without differentiation, within a conventional risk model, runs the risk of coming up with results insignificantly different from zero.[56] Therefore, as far as possible, this monograph attempts to distinguish between studies focusing on different styles of SRI portfolio.

---

[56]This problem is also raised by Diltz (1995), who refers to the many varieties of SRI funds.

Exhibit 5.3. Summary: SRI Approaches and Relevant Tests of Financial Performance

SRI Approach	Portfolio Characteristics	Relevant Performance Test
Exclusion	Return to risk deteriorates in the short run because of reduction in diversification. Pure exclusion portfolios are not constructed with the aim of delivering alpha; the investor is prepared to pay a price to support social beliefs.	Benchmark-relative performance irrelevant, at least in the short run. May be more relevant in the long run (but it is not clear how to test for this).
Exclusion + best-in-class hybrid	Diversified active portfolio: Under the assumption that manager skill is present, gains from active strategy (portfolio tilted to strong "social" performers) offset by cost of reduced diversification (exclusion).	Over the long run, a properly risk-adjusted conventional financial model. In the short run, expect divergence—how much being dependent on the weight of exclusions in the portfolio. See above.
Best in class	Diversified active portfolio strategy with the aim of enhancing performance in the long run.	A properly risk-adjusted conventional financial model. Note that there may be some "style" bias (e.g., best-in-class funds may be similar to value funds in terms of risk profile).
Best in class + engagement hybrid	Active diversified portfolio with some concentrated positions to permit shareholder to act as owner where relevant. Cost of lower diversification offset by stronger monitoring.	Over the long run, a properly risk-adjusted conventional financial model. In the short run, expect divergence.
Engagement	Shareholder acts as owner. Risk reduction (and return enhancement) expected to arise from close relationship between shareholder and firm (under the assumption that markets are not strong form efficient) and not from portfolio diversification.	If engagement portfolios are highly concentrated, the use of normal performance benchmarks may overstate portfolio risks. (Risk is reduced through monitoring, which is not reflected in the benchmark if a market proxy is used.)
Advocacy/Activism	Shareholder acts as owner. Portfolio not necessarily concentrated in few stocks. Risk reduction from a combination of diversification and monitoring.	A properly risk-adjusted conventional financial model.

Portfolio Performance Studies in Action

The analysis of the impact of SRI approaches on portfolio performance can be undertaken in three ways:

1. analyze cross-sections of the reported portfolio returns of existing investment vehicles, such as mutual funds in the United States or open-ended investment companies (OEICs) in Europe,

2. analyze the risk characteristics and return attribution of individual portfolios on the basis of the constituent stock holdings, and

3. create portfolios on the basis of screened universes of stocks with a view to constructing performance back-tests.

The following sections attempt to segment fund studies by fund type where possible (exclusion, best in class, engagement), and within each of these sections, cross-sectional, stock-based, and synthetic portfolio approaches are identified.

Performance of Negative Screening or Exclusion Portfolios.
As would be expected, mutual fund performance studies deliver mixed results. A study by Girard, Stone, and Rahman (2005), in which they applied the appropriate style benchmarks to a database of 117 U.S. socially responsible mutual funds, found that for the 1984–2003 period, socially responsible mutual fund managers showed "poor selectivity, net selectivity, and market timing ability" and, in addition, found evidence of diversification costs.[57] Gregory, Matatko, and Luther (1997) obtained similar results after adjusting for fund size and furthermore found that the more constrained the fund (the larger the number of screens), the lower performance to net selectivity. Kreander, Gray, Power, and Sinclair (2005) compared the performance of pairs of ethical and nonethical funds matched for age, size, country, and investment universe and found no significant difference in performance between peer groups on the basis of several measures (the Sharpe ratio, Jensen's alpha, the Treynor measure).

Statman (2000) reviewed the performance of a group of 31 socially screened equity mutual funds for the May 1990 to September 1998 time period by using Jensen's alpha and a modified Sharpe ratio. He found that socially responsible mutual funds, on average, underperform their benchmarks (whether the S&P 500 or the Domini Social Index). But their performance was no worse than the average performance of conventional funds (p. 34). Bauer, Koedijk, and Otten (2002) applied a multifactor model to analyze "ethical" fund performance of 103 German, U.K., and U.S. ethical mutual fund equivalents. After controlling for investment style, the authors found little evidence of significant differences in risk-adjusted returns between ethical and conventional funds for the 1990–2001 period. In the same study, the introduction of time variation in betas revealed significant underperformance of domestic U.S. funds and a significant outperformance of U.K. ethical funds, relative to their conventional peers. Finally, they documented a learning effect.

Elsewhere, a similar analysis by Bauer, Otten, and Rad (2004) based on a model controlling for investment style, time variation in betas, bond exposure, and home bias found no evidence of significant differences in risk-adjusted returns between

---

[57]A list of the funds in the database is given in the article. The funds are described in terms of their mainstream style (growth, value, etc.) but not in terms of their SRI style. It is likely, however, that most of the funds are exclusion funds.

                    ©2006, The Research Foundation of CFA Institute

ethical and conventional funds in Australia. Overall, for studies that appear to focus mostly on exclusion funds, the results seem to vary between negative performance results, to no difference, to positive performance in some situations when full adjustments are made for market, sector, style, size, and momentum effects.

In an interesting piece of work by Geczy, Stambaugh, and Levin (2003), the authors constructed "funds of funds" by building optimal portfolios of funds selected from a universe of U.S. SRI funds. They noted that the cost of imposing an SRI constraint depends strongly on the mutual fund investor's beliefs about pricing models and manager skill (p. 3). They found that where a market-index investor—one who believes strongly in the capital asset pricing model (CAPM) and who rules out managerial skill—selects SRI funds from a broad universe of such funds (both exclusion and positive screening) with the aim of replicating a mainstream passive index, the cost of the SRI constraint is typically just a few basis points a month. For the investor selecting from pure exclusion (defined as screening out stocks in typically excluded industries) and believing in risk models, such as the single-factor CAPM, the cost of the SRI constraint is around a few basis points, whereas for the believer in Fama–French (1993) or Carhart (1997) models, it is around 10 bps. For an investor choosing SRI funds from a mixed universe of SRI approaches and disallowing manager skill but accepting pricing models incorporating size, value, and momentum factors, the costs of an SRI constraint can be much higher.

A further study indicated that the way in which screens are implemented at the level of the portfolio—with or without portfolio optimization techniques—may have an impact on performance. Troutman (2001) described a portfolio risk analysis case study (the Evangelical Lutheran Church in America [ELCA] Board of Pensions U.S. equity portfolios). The screens applied were weapons and harmful products and energy and environment. His work indicates that exclusion had only very moderate impact on fund risk characteristics. The author observed, however, that

> Without optimization techniques, simply replicating the constrained universe would have generated much greater deviations from the returns of the unconstrained Russell 3000 benchmark portfolio. (p. 54)

In short, the substitution trades that are made to replace excluded stocks affect the expected return to risk.

A number of significant studies create synthetic exclusion portfolios. These include the work of Guerard (1997) and Stone, Guerard, Gultekin, and Adams (2001). The study by Guerard (1997) involved the construction of stock portfolios on the basis of an application of screens provided by KLD in the following: military, nuclear power, product (alcohol, tobacco, and gambling), and environment. For returns data between January 1987 and December 1994, no evidence of a screening performance penalty was apparent. Stone et al. (2001) extended the work of Guerard (1997), incorporating adjustments for beta, growth, size (market capitalization), and dividend yield. This addition made no difference to the conclusion. Neither study found any significant difference in the performance of screened and unscreened universes of stocks. The systematic application of quantitative models is noteworthy in both studies.

This section is not complete without considering the "opposite pole" of opinion. A recent article by Hemley, Morris, and Gilde (2005) examined the performance of sectors typically excluded from SRI funds (tobacco, gambling, and alcohol) and found that they all performed better than the benchmark over an 11-year period. Even if SRI screens do contain signaling information with respect to long-run social and (eventually) market trends, it would appear that this investment approach is no different from any other. At times, it will underperform (and at times outperform) the benchmark.

Performance of SRI Best-in-Class Portfolios. Best-in-class SRI portfolio approaches generally consist of ranking companies on the basis of environmental, social, ethical, and governance criteria prior to constraining the investment universe at a suitable cut-off point in the ranking and then constructing a portfolio on the basis of required return and risk appetite in the normal way. This literature search did not manage to identify many mutual fund studies based purely on best-in-class funds; therefore, the focus is on work based on the construction of synthetic portfolios.

Diltz (1995) constructed 14 paired portfolios (for each factor, a portfolio of stocks rated "good" and a portfolio of stocks rated "poor") based on social criteria of the Council on Economic Priorities (CEP). On the basis of market-model alphas and abnormal returns, no significant difference in returns was found. Significant findings include superior performance of several of the poorly rated portfolios and outperformance of the highly rated portfolios at times when the issue in question had a high profile in the press. Cohen, Fenn, and Konar (1997) created two baskets of firms—firms having low and high scores, respectively, on measures of environmental performance—and found that a strategy of choosing the environmental leaders in an industry-balanced portfolio did as well (or better) than the environmental laggards in each industry. Derwall et al. (2005) applied a best-in-class approach to build "eco-efficiency" portfolios, eco-efficiency being defined as the ratio of the "value a company adds (e.g., by producing products) to the waste the company generates by creating that value." The mean return of the best-in-class portfolios was 13 percent, versus 9.9 percent for the worst between July 1995 and December 2003.

On a slightly different note, Milevsky, Aziz, Goss, Thomson, and Wheeler (2004) focused on good and bad employment practices, running simulated portfolios on the basis of exclusions of "worst in class" firms, or those scoring low on "good practice" rankings. They illustrated that portfolio optimization can be used to locate statistical portfolio substitutes for investments and companies that fail a CSR screen to a sufficient extent to eliminate significant diversification costs.

No empirical work based on engagement or activist portfolios was identified.

Indices

A summary of the main index construction methodologies is found in Chapter 1, Exhibit 1.4. The key point about SRI indices is that they represent quite different investment philosophies and approaches; therefore, any analysis of them says something about only the specific approach rather than SRI in general. Overall, analytical work based on the indices leads to the same conclusions as the work based on portfolios and stock baskets: The performance impact of SRI policy on indices does not appear to be (statistically) significantly different from zero. There does appear to be an increased cost in the sense that tracking error relative to traditional benchmarks can be significant. Whether this matters, however, ultimately depends on the return requirements, market beliefs, and risk appetite of the investor, as discussed in Chapter 1. A study by Statman (2005b) looked at the constituents, returns, and tracking error of the Domini 400 Social Index (DS 400 Index), the Calvert Social Index, the Citizens Index, and the U.S. portion of the Dow Jones Sustainability Indexes versus the S&P 500. Jensen's alpha, the Sharpe ratio, and the Fama and French three-factor model were used to compare the indices. The returns of the DS 400 Index were higher than those of the S&P 500, although differences were not statistically significant. Elsewhere, Statman (2000, Table 1) reviewed the performance of the Domini Social Index (DSI) between May 1990 and September 1998 and found that the DSI's risk-adjusted returns for this period were higher than those of the S&P 500. An earlier study by Sauer (1997) concluded:

> A comparison of the raw and risk-adjusted performance of the DSI with two unrestricted, well diversified benchmark portfolios suggests that application of social responsibility screens does not necessarily have an adverse impact on investment performance. Regardless of the market proxy selected, the empirical evidence indicates that the potential performance costs of implementing social responsibility criteria, as represented by the performance of the DSI, are negligible. (p. 137)

Kurtz and diBartolomeo (2005) analyzed the performance of the Catholic Values 400 Index. They used the Northfield Fundamental U.S. Equity Factor Model in their analysis and found that the index had a higher beta, lower market capitalization, and higher valuation ratios than the S&P 500 and no significant difference in return between 1998 and 2004. Hussein and Omran (2005) examined the performance of Islamic indices between 1995 and 2000 and found outperformance during bull markets, underperformance during bear markets, and cumulatively, outperformance relative to Dow Jones benchmarks. Vermeir, Van de Velde, and Corten (2005) examined the performance (absolute and risk adjusted) of a range of sustainability indices—ASPI-Index (Vigeo), ESIE and ESIG (Ethibel), Dow Jones Sustainability (Dow Jones SAM), Domini Social Index (KLD), FTSE4Good (FTSE)—and concluded that sustainable screening does not have to come at the expense of poorer risk–return characteristics.

Summary

This chapter has reviewed some of the literature on the impact of environmental and social performance on corporate profitability, share price performance and valuation, and portfolio and SRI index performance. For corporate performance, the question posed was whether investment in environmental or social performance adds or destroys value. The answer appears to depend on the competitive structure of markets, but on balance, firms that compete to be best in class in all areas, including in their environmental and social performance, appear to outperform, with the usual caveats about survivorship bias in the data (and publication bias in empirical studies). For share price performance, there is little doubt that CSR issues can and do affect share prices. The more important point, however, is that some markers of environmental performance, in particular, appear to signal potential anomalies in financial (as well as social) terms.

At the level of the portfolio, where systematic portfolio risk overlays were in place, the findings were consistently that exclusion need make no significant difference. For best-in class-portfolios, the indications are consistent with some of the event-study research on stocks: It appears that some markers of environmental and social performance may signal financial market anomalies; in other words, they may contain information that is not always in the market. This hypothesis is impossible to prove, but it is worth considering the following. SRI (along with economic regulation) is often about the internalization of externalized costs, and indeed, some SRI practitioners look actively for means to crystallize such costs in a corporate context (see Chapter 1 and Chapter 3). SRI as a discipline, therefore, appears well positioned to watch for return drivers that are, initially, irrelevant to financial markets but may become so.

 ©2006, The Research Foundation of CFA Institute

6. Putting SRI into a Theoretical Context

This chapter is not intended to be an exhaustive survey of the theory of finance.[58] Rather, it considers two areas: (1) whether any accepted theoretical frameworks provide a rationale for socially responsible investment as a portfolio approach and (2) where the concerns encountered in previous chapters fit into risk models widely used in the field of finance.[59]

With respect to the first question, earlier chapters have thrown some light on such issues. Chapter 2 explored the relevance of economic welfare to SRI in the sense that investors maximize returns subject to values-based constraints. Chapters 2 and 5 explored the relationship between externalities and markets and made a brief mention of the free-rider problem. Chapter 2 suggested that the adoption of a socially responsible investment approach involves a rejection of "efficiency" somewhere in the system, a possibility explored in later pages (see also Exhibits 5.1 and 5.2). And Chapter 5 explored a number of research papers in which information discovered in research areas relevant to SRI appeared to be incorporated in asset prices with a lag and, therefore, in which the semi-strong form of the efficient market hypothesis appeared not to hold.

The second question can be addressed from the basis of building-block valuation approaches widely used in finance: Either a firm may be valued on the basis of an estimation of the net present value of future equity cash flows, or a firm may be valued on the basis of the market value of all the claims on the firm's business (usually called the "residual claims" approach). In the context of the residual claims approach, note that SRI issues may, having not been relevant, become relevant as information becomes more easily (cheaply) obtainable or simply relevant where it previously was not because of catalyst events, such as regulatory change. As shown previously, event risk is highly relevant in the context of SRI. On this basis, it is worth considering that options-based contingent claims approaches may at some stage become relevant to SRI; however, the practical difficulties of implementing such approaches would be considerable. Finally, earlier sections considered what beliefs might drive the four main approaches to SRI identified in this work (see **Exhibit 6.1** for a summary). The question is whether any rationale exists for SRI in the context of portfolio theory.

---

[58] As with Chapter 2, an inevitable element of idea exploration also exists in this chapter, which means more questions may be raised than fully answered. The approach, however, is emphatically empirical.
[59] With thanks to James Sefton for his help with some of the ideas in this section.

Exhibit 6.1. Recap: Four Approaches

The exclusion approach is often regarded as quite far removed from conventional approaches to portfolio management, which dictate managing the portfolio to generate the maximum return to risk. Exclusion approaches fly in the face of this logic, apparently entailing an acceptance of a suboptimal return to risk by forgoing the full benefits of diversification. Values-based exclusion portfolios are not necessarily constructed with the aim of delivering alpha. In short, the investor must be prepared to pay a price to support social beliefs.

Best-in-class approaches fit easily into existing stock and/or security selection and risk control processes, particularly if it is believed that environmental, social, and governance issues have financial impact. After all, it is common practice to constrain the investment universe on the basis of sector, country or region, and style.[a] The best-in-class portfolio can be described as a diversified active portfolio strategy with the aim of enhancing performance in the long run by tilting the portfolio toward strong all-round (financial and social) performers.

In the engagement approach, portfolio performance is expected to be positively affected by the direct influence of the owner on companies in the portfolio and, therefore, on the performance of the portfolio. Portfolio risk reduction is expected to arise from the close relationship between shareholder and firm and not (necessarily) from portfolio diversification.

Advocacy/activism can be described as organized support of a specific cause. It is not necessarily the same as engagement because this approach involves acting as a group. Some may see activism as a first step; and others may see it as the next step if engagement (defined as a two-way dialog between shareholder and firm) does not have the desired effect. In practice, there may thus be some overlap between the approaches.

[a]Typical constraints, or screens, include growth, value, size, dividend payout levels, and financial leverage.

Economic or Financial Economic Rationale for SRI

Taking the first question (the rationale for SRI, if any, as an approach) first, the following sections review the relevance of welfare economics, externalities, the free-rider problem, and the presence of research costs (where appropriate) in the context of the four approaches.

Welfare Economics and Other Points. The efficient market hypothesis (EMH) implies that all investors are rational mean–variance optimizers; that is, they seek to maximize return to risk (or minimize the risk associated with any given asset return) at all times. Therefore, all investors will hold the market portfolio, subject to given assumptions. As established, maximizing return to risk within constraints determined by individual utilities may, at times, be a better description of investor behavior, which is where welfare economics (along with the associated disciplines of development economics and regulation economics) as a framework can become relevant.

This aspect of theoretical support for negative exclusion approaches needs no further explanation beyond the material in Chapters 1 and 2. Either the value judgment behind the constraint is accepted or it is not by the relevant investor. But two important points need to be emphasized in this context. First, the significance of exclusions as signaling information should not be ignored, particularly when

©2006, The Research Foundation of CFA Institute

exclusions are implemented as a cohort. Values-based constraints followed by individuals can be expected to have little or no market impact. Constraints followed by an eventual majority (or even a large minority) may do so. How this situation can be expected to play out, then, depends on which of two theoretical frameworks—the free-rider problem or market efficiency approaches—may turn out to be the better explanation of market behavior.

The free-rider problem in the specific context of exclusion portfolios suggests that asset managers running portfolios without any values-driven stock, country, or sector constraints may benefit at the expense of portfolios invested with such exclusions. If it is assumed, for example, that companies engaged in commercial activity in typical SRI exclusion areas profit from this activity and if it is further assumed that this "profit" is reflected in asset prices, then by avoiding such assets, exclusion portfolios may lose out. Furthermore, exclusion portfolios can be said to pass a direct benefit to those who hold different (opposite) beliefs and who (by implication) choose to be free riders.

In contrast, market inefficiency approaches suggest that the "free ride" may potentially turn out not to have been free but paid for by an unrecognized risk exposure. In short, the risk to investors in sectors typically avoided by ethical investors is that the relevant social cost becomes internalized, resulting in increased asset price volatility and perhaps even in an outright fall in share prices. Such an effect appears to have been observed by the authors of work referred to in Chapter 5.

Which of the two approaches is correct is impossible to say (markets are the ultimate arbiter here!). And therefore, ultimately, it comes down to the main decision driver of the investment decision maker in the chain (and his or her values) and the goal of maximizing portfolio returns within values-based constraints.

Externalities and the Free-Rider Problem.[60] As discussed previously, it is highly unlikely that all assets and liabilities—including environmental, social, governance, and ethical assets and liabilities—are reflected in the market at all times. This supposition is difficult to prove, but it seems reasonable to hypothesize that some of the assets and liabilities recognized in the context of so-called green accounts (UN, EC, IMF, OECD, and World Bank 2003; Hamilton and Lutz 1996) may be a good analogy for corporate assets and liabilities, or economic costs and benefits, not being recognized at certain times in financial markets. It is, in general, well recognized that return measures used by governments, firms, and other bodies—or in the context of traditional economics, accounting profit, and

---

[60]To avoid confusion, note that the free-rider problem is discussed in two contexts: (1) Those investing in industries excluded from a significant number of SRI portfolios can be said to be "free riding" if it is indeed the case that the portfolio reflects profits gained on the basis of externalized costs. (2) Those enjoying the benefits of the work of engagement investors, without putting in engagement efforts themselves, can be said to be free riding on research costs sustained by others.

cash flow—may mask economic inefficiency or, conversely, may give a false appearance of inefficiency. What is reflected in the market at any time is likely to change, indicating that assets and liabilities that at one given moment appear to have no financial relevance may do so later. In all likelihood, in the past, before the arrival of specific environmental regulations in many countries, environmental issues had very little impact on the profitability or valuation of firms (and thus little impact on equity markets). It is impossible to ascertain whether markets took this into account and "priced in" a probability-weighted future cost of environmental damage at the time; it is more likely that markets simply extrapolated forward from the earnings stream of the time, ignoring the "noncash" costs of environmental pollution and the relative performance of firms in this area.

Thus, active portfolio managers selecting firms on the basis of environmental performance before the regulations arrived may have had a lead on investors who did not use such criteria when the regulations took effect (although before then, of course, they were taking market-relative risk and had no way of knowing when a relevant catalyst for change would arrive). The apparently anomalous incorporation of environmental information in equity returns with drift, identified in some of the research reviewed in Chapter 5,[61] may, in fact, be explained by something like the incorporation of information that initially was either not known or disregarded as irrelevant over a period of time. At this juncture, the presence of engagement and activist investors in the SRI arena becomes important. Chapter 1 noted the significant amount of collaborative activity by SRI specialists. In this light, a suggestion made by Admati et al. (1994) as a fruitful avenue for future research may be relevant: They suggested the possibility of the presence of specialist monitors who might hold a different portfolio from the market portfolio (p. 1124).[62] Chapter 2 referred to a body of literature on the value of institutional investor monitoring. Overall, it appears the rationale for activist and engagement approaches to SRI is two-fold: the presence of externalities in the context of social and environmental issues and the presence of the free-rider problem with respect to research and engagement costs. One outcome of either approach may be to act as a trigger for internalization of the relevant environmental or social costs.

Presence of Information Search Costs. A huge body of literature explores market efficiency. In this context, the information search undertaken by the SRI community can be considered in the context of the seminal work of Grossman and Stiglitz (1980). Their argument suggests that asset prices reflect information known to arbitrageurs but not completely, allowing those who expend

---

[61]See Derwall, Guenster, Bauer, and Koedijk (2005).

[62]Smaller investors would be able to hold the market portfolio by holding these specialist funds with others.

research resources to be compensated for the cost of the information search. Chapter 5 contained what appears to be a good example relating to an issue that market participants have been able to become better informed about as time has passed in the form of empirical work in the area of eco-efficiency based on a version of the market model incorporating a size effect (Banz 1981; Reinganum 1981) in the early 1980s; a value/growth stock effect (Fama and French 1993)[63] in the early to mid-1990s; and a momentum factor (Carhart 1997) in the 1990s, known as the Carhart model:

$$R_s - R_f = \alpha + \beta\left(R_m - R_f\right) + \beta_2 SMB + \beta_3 HML + \beta_4 MOM,$$

where

$R_s - R_f$ = excess return of the relevant asset
α = return to specific risk
β = sensitivity of the asset to the market
$R_m - R_f$ = excess return of "the market" over the risk-free rate
SMB = return difference between a small-cap and a large-cap portfolio
HML = return difference between a value portfolio and a growth portfolio
MOM = return difference between a portfolio of winners and losers over a 12-month interval

Derwall et al. (2005) used this model to assess the performance of stock portfolios consisting of large-cap firms labeled "most eco-efficient" and "least eco-efficient" and found a significant performance difference. The results of this study seem to suggest that eco-efficiency may have been a significant source of alpha, or return not explained within the risk model over the time period in question. From the Grossman–Stiglitz (1980) perspective, the excess return captured here could be regarded as compensation for research costs.

An alternative explanation may, however, be risk based. One possible hypothesis is that eco-efficiency is a further factor not included in the version of the model shown above. Of course, this added "factor" may just become incorporated within the "market" factor as environmental risk becomes an internalized cost for firms. As seen in previous sections, catalysts that might bring about an incorporation of environmental or social risk within "market risk" can include changes in regulation, investor preference, and other behavioral and social change. In this case, the externality approach is the possible explanation for results of the study. As these paragraphs suggest, the precise mechanism by which SRI issues drive returns is unclear. It seems reasonable to suppose that they fit somewhere; it is just not clear where.

---

[63]Book-to-market equity is a proxy for valuation and a marker for "value" versus "growth" stocks.

Exhibit 6.2 summarizes the main portfolio characteristics for the four SRI approaches and includes an indication of the most relevant theoretical rationale for the approach.

Valuation and SRI

The second question looks at SRI in the context of widely used valuation models. A well-recognized maxim of modern finance is that one of the best ways of estimating a firm's ability to generate future cash flow is to value it (Black 1980). A firm that is highly valued in financial markets will have the greatest flexibility with respect to sources of cash: Should free cash flow not be available in the short run,

Exhibit 6.2. SRI Approaches and Supporting Theoretical Frameworks

SRI Approach	Portfolio Characteristics	Supporting Theory
Exclusion	Return to financial risk may deteriorate in the short run because of reduction in diversification. Pure exclusion portfolios are not constructed with the aim of delivering alpha.	With the main concern being to maximize returns within values-based constraints, the relevant supporting theory can be said to be welfare economics.
		Theory running counter to this approach: the free-rider problem (see Derwall et al. 2005) but note that exclusion approaches implemented by a cohort may overcome this problem.
Best in class	The diversified active portfolio strategy has the aim of enhancing performance in the long run.	With the main concern being to capture outperformance driven by social and economic "factors," the most relevant supporting theory can be said to be the presence of costly information and the associated Grossman–Stiglitz (1980) paradox.[a]
Engagement	Shareholder acts as owner. Risk reduction (and return enhancement) expected to arise from close relationship between shareholder and firm (under the assumption that markets are not strong form efficient) and not from portfolio diversification.	The main concern is to capture returns generated through a collaborative relationship between owner and manager. Monitoring reduces risk. Ownership structure affects firm payoffs (Admati et al. 1994). May assist internalization of externalized costs.
Advocacy	Underlying portfolio can be active or passive, diversified or concentrated.	This approach can be said to tackle the (social) free-rider problem head on (by moving to internalize economic, environmental, and social externalities) as well as the market free-rider problem encountered in the context of engagement.

[a]If markets were efficient, investors would have no incentive to expend time and effort searching for information.

©2006, The Research Foundation of CFA Institute

external sources would be far more readily available to firms having high stock market valuations than the reverse. SRI is most obviously relevant to valuation when it is likely that environmental, social, or ethical issues may compromise the future ability of the firm to generate cash. Such issues, however, can be relevant to the generation of cash in many ways. For example, how they are handled may affect operating efficiency, operational risk, competitive positioning, or brand strength. The relationship between valuation and SRI is not a simple, straightforward matter.

The research papers reviewed in Chapter 5 identified several approaches to valuation in the context of SRI. One approach is to calculate the net present value of a firm's cash flows to obtain an absolute value, with a view to testing the impact of different input assumptions, such as the work of Repetto and Austin (2000), Austin and Sauer (2002), and Austin, Rosinski, Sauer, and le Duc (2003). Another approach is to observe share price reactions to specific events, as in the work of Filbeck and Gorman (2004), Govindaraj et al. (2004), Dasgupta et al. (1997), and Hamilton (1995). And yet another approach is to look at the impact of differential CSR performance on valuation, most usually on firms' price-to-book ratios or q ratios as seen, for example, in the work of Dowell et al. (2000), Guenster et al. (2005), and Khanna et al. (2004).

The following paragraphs will briefly review each of these approaches, in turn, relating them to the relevant financial theory where possible.

Discounted Cash Flow Approaches. In discounted cash flow approaches, the value of the firm is defined as the present value of its future cash flows, CF, discounted at the firm's weighted-average cost of capital, r. The market value of *nonequity claims*, such as debt, can be subtracted from this number to arrive at the firm's equity value, V:

$$V = \sum_{t=1}^{t=n} \frac{CF_t}{(1+r)^t}. \tag{6.1}$$

An alternative to valuing the firm's equity, V_E, is to take the net present value of equity cash flows, ECF. In this case, equity cash flows are taken net of *cash flows attributable to other claimants* and discounted at the cost of equity, k:

$$V_E = \sum_{t=1}^{t=n} \frac{ECF_t}{(1+k_e)^t}. \tag{6.2}$$

This well-known formula begs two questions in the context of SRI. Nonequity cash flows usually consist of those relating to debt and other liabilities. Nonequity claims could, clearly, also include environmental or social liabilities or alternatively might be offset by environmental or social assets. The question is how to deal with any such obligations not necessarily recognized by the firm in financial statements (as discussed in Chapter 4, accounting conventions may not permit their inclusion) but which the analyst believes may appear as cash flows (either negative or positive) in the medium term. The answer proposed is that if the analyst believes the firm's future cash flows may be affected by environmental, social, or governance issues, then they should be reflected in the relevant discounted cash flow model (Equation 6.1 or 6.2) either at the level of equity cash flows (net of nonequity cash flows) or in the cost of equity, or perhaps both. So, clearly, the presence of positive cash flows associated with environmental, social, and governance issues may enhance the equity value of the firm, and conversely, the presence of cash flows away from equity to other claimants could reduce the value of the firm's equity (see also Hudson 2005). One problem facing analysts attempting to construct such models is that many environmental and social costs are often not identifiable or quantifiable (see Chapter 4), and so in practical terms, building even reasonably accurate models may be impossible. Examples appear in **Exhibit 6.3**. Once a relevant regulatory or market mechanism has been introduced, it becomes much easier to incorporate environmental and social costs into models. For "social" issues, such as diversity in the workforce or the use of child labor, where quantified costs are not present, the analyst has to decide individually how to implement the impact within the model. As Exhibit 6.3 shows, no clearly accepted methodology exists. But exactly the same problems are encountered in the modeling of intangibles.

Exhibit 6.3.   Incorporating Environmental and Social Issues into Financial Models

Impact	Impact on Firm	Hypothetical Costs with Potential to Cause Financial Distress
Pollution incident	Cleanup costs. Fines. Lawsuits. Damage to reputation.	Cash outflow: If substantial, financial distress. Firm's risk profile: If higher (either financially or operationally), WACC will rise.
Nondiverse workforce	Performance of nondiverse workforce possibly suboptimal. Reaction of workforce may result in direct costs (recruitment costs to replace staff, potential lawsuits).	Lower cash flow, or at the extreme, cash outflow. Reputational impact, difficulty in hiring. In the extreme, cost of capital effects.
Global warming	With emission restrictions: carbon costs.	Carbon costs (benefits) are cash outflows (inflows) in the short term and potential liabilities in the long run.
Consumer reaction against use of child labor	Opportunity cost.	Reputational impact.

            ©2006, The Research Foundation of CFA Institute

The next question is what discount rate should be applied to the relevant cash flows, particularly those arising in the medium to long term. The usual procedure is to apply the weighted-average cost of capital to the total cash flows of the firm (enterprise) and the cost of equity to equity cash flows. The WACC is usually calculated according to the following well-known formula:

$$\text{WACC} = k_D \left(1 - T_C\right)\left(\frac{D}{E+D}\right) + k_E \left(\frac{E}{E+D}\right), \tag{6.3}$$

where D equals the firm's total debt, E equals the firm's total equity, and T equals the tax rate.

The firm's WACC is likely to be affected by the presence of substantial environmental, social, or governance risk, which might happen through one of several mechanisms. The firm's equity risk premium might rise because of the higher risk attached to equity cash flows. A hypothetical alternative, which certainly raises far more questions than it answers, might be to think of the WACC as shown in Equation 6.4, reflecting the presence of a cost of obligations and applying a specific discount rate, or a "social discount rate" k_{SOC}, to environmental and social obligations as well as to the equity and debt claims. In this case, the firm's WACC might be calculated as follows:

$$\text{WACC} = k_D \left(1 - T_C\right)\left(\frac{D}{E+D+SOC}\right) + k_E \left(\frac{E}{E+D+SOC}\right) + k_{SOC} \left(\frac{SOC}{E+D+SOC}\right). \tag{6.4}$$

Note that the above equation has not appeared in any body of finance theory this author has seen, for good reasons: Defining "social capital" or "environmental capital" may require quite different approaches depending on whether such capital is renewable or a wasting asset, and so Equation 6.4 would not fit all situations. What it does, however, is to raise a critical point: This is what the social discount rate should be. Note, in particular, the potential impact of a *low* social discount rate applied to environmental or social claims on the value of equity calculated (*net* of these other claims), as shown in Equation 6.1.

The question of the social discount rate has been widely aired. Some argue that the firm's WACC "is a good approximation of the true social discount rate" (Boardman, Greenberg, Vining, and Weimer 2001, p. 238). Others argue that the social discount rate should be zero[64] because environmental and social liabilities often arise a long way in the future[65]—in which case the net present value of the obligation

---

[64]Frank Ramsey, Cambridge philosopher 1903–30, is one such person. He also made groundbreaking contributions to the field of subjective probability, choice under uncertainty, the theory of taxation (Boiteux–Ramsey model), and optimal growth (the Ramsey model). See the History of Economic Thought website at http://homepage.newschool.edu/het/.

[65]The theory that explains the phenomenon of low long-term discount rates is called the "bequest motive." See, for example, Frederick, Loewenstein, and O'Donoghue (2002).

is the same as its nominal value today. Other solutions to the problem of defining the social discount for very long-term liabilities fall somewhere between the extremes (WACC versus 0 percent) and include using the marginal social rate of time preference, the weighted social opportunity cost of capital, and the shadow price of capital.[66] The other question is which discount rate is applied over time. The simple equity model above (Equations 6.1–6.2) suggests that one discount rate is applied to all the firm's future cash flows. Of course, in practice, discount rates can and do vary with time, and some analyst models apply the prevailing yield curve to cash flows, varying the rate over specific years. It has been suggested that social discount rates may decline over time.[67] For example, a survey of 2,160 economists with respect to the relevant discount in an environmental context suggested that 4 percent should apply over 1–5 years, 3 percent over 6–25 years, 2 percent over 26–75 years, 1 percent between 76 and 200 years, and zero after that (Weitzman 1994). As discussed, a low (even zero) social discount rate in the long run, applied to social or environmental claims, would clearly be significant in the context of Equations 6.1–6.2.

It must be stressed that the above framing of the WACC is purely exploratory, having no basis in any theory seen by the author. It is purely a construct intended to make a point about the potential impact of social and environmental issues on the value of the firm. This monograph will return to the discount rate question in the context of residual claims below.

Share Price Reactions to New Information. As shown earlier, those looking to identify share price reactions to new information generally follow event study methodology. Such studies are a direct test of the efficient market hypothesis, as observed in Chapter 5. Several studies found that, in risk-adjusted terms, information appeared to be incorporated with a lag. This finding may be consistent with the "information" theories mentioned previously, or an alternative explanation might be sought in the anomaly approach of behavioral finance. The increasing availability of information in some areas—particularly relating to environmental performance—may, however, simply be making arbitrage possible where it was not before. In the medium term, as markets become more efficient in response to better information flows, the market should find equilibrium where arbitrage profits just cover research costs.

---

[66]The MRTP (marginal social rate of time preference) is the interest rate at which people are willing to postpone a small amount of present consumption in exchange for additional future consumption. The WSOC (weighted social opportunity cost of capital) is the social opportunity cost of resources used to fund the relevant project, each weighted in proportion to its contribution. In the SPC (shadow price of capital), gains or losses are converted into consumption equivalents, which are then discounted at the marginal social rate of time preference.

[67]Note that in 1928, Ramsey posited one discount rate; otherwise, it would be possible to arbitrage across time, as quoted in Paxson (1995).

©2006, The Research Foundation of CFA Institute

Valuation Ratios. The price-to-book ratio is widely used by equity analysts largely because it is an obtainable, well-understood, and reasonably stable metric and also because, unlike the DCF approach discussed previously, it is less subject to variance in the input assumptions, particularly the discount rate, which is not easily defined. In addition, the well-known relationship between the price-to-book ratio and ROE makes it particularly suited to situations in which the analyst is trying to understand the impact of company behavior on accounting profit and, as a next step, the extent to which it is reflected in valuation.[68] As seen in Chapter 5, a number of authors have taken this two-step approach in the context of SRI research. The CSR performance of the company (relating to environmental performance, social performance, and governance practices) is widely believed by SRI practitioners to have an impact on a firm's fundamental (financial) performance through its ability to generate return on equity and also an impact on its risk as reflected in the firm's cost of funds.

SRI practitioners also believe that a firm's CSR performance has an impact on its intangible value. Tobin's q ratio is calculated as the market value of the claims of the business (usually the sum of the market value of debt and equity) divided by the replacement value of the firm's business assets. To the extent that the q ratio is above 1, the firm has succeeded in creating intangible value. In practice, estimating the q ratio is fraught with practical difficulties. For instance, obtaining the replacement value of a firm's business assets is likely to be impossible in most cases. Quite often, a shortcut is taken, and the q ratio becomes analogous to the price-to-book ratio: The market value of the firm's claims is divided by the book value of its claims. In general, however, given the beliefs of SRI practitioners mentioned previously, the q ratio is considered a measure of value creation that is well aligned with research objectives, which are to capture economic value created by the way firms handle CSR issues.[69]

Residual Claims Approach. The value of a firm may be calculated from one of two perspectives. Starting from asset markets, it may be defined as the market value of all claims on the business. Alternatively, starting with a firm's cash flows, it may be calculated as the net present value of cash flows, as discussed above.[70] In equilibrium, either approach should give the same answer. These two perspectives are shown in **Exhibit 6.4,** with market values on the left and cash flows on the right, but to each column an environmental/social dimension has been added so that a wider range of stakeholders is represented in the model (equity claimants, debt

---

[68]The price-to-book ratio is an increasing function of the firm's ROE, payout ratio, and growth rate and declines with the increasing riskiness of the firm.

[69]The work of Lindenberg and Ross (1981), who break down the value of the firm into "tangible" and "intangible" values, is also relevant in this context.

[70]This idea was explored in Hudson (2005), and the help of Stephen Cooper is gratefully acknowledged in the development of the idea.

Exhibit 6.4. SRI Firm Value

Liabilities or "Claims" on the Business	Cash Flows
Equity	Dividends, other cash remaining to shareholders
Debt	Interest and principal and other relevant cash flows
Environmental and social (e.g., a known requirement to make good a depleted asset)[a]	Cash flows generated by the environmental and social assets of the business (e.g., access to some raw materials having social value)

[a]It is not known whether these are reflected in market prices. The assumption here is that they are present, (everything) is priced, but they are not usually separated out or "visible."

Source: Based on Hudson (2005).

claimants, and "social" claimants). The corporation has frequently been described as a nexus of contracts, written and unwritten, among owners of factors of production and the many other stakeholders involved in the firm, including the providers of finance.[71] In Exhibit 6.4, this "nexus" is intended to be more completely represented than in conventional financial models, although for the sake of clarity, it has been reduced to just three "contracts." In the owner-managed firm, the cash flows net of all costs flow back to the owner. If ownership and control are separated,[72] as they are for many companies, this residual risk is generally borne by shareholders,[73] but if any of the contracts are broken or rewritten (as in bankruptcy or in the redefining of corporate pension fund benefits) many more parties may be subject to residual risk because available cash flows net of claims having a higher priority may be quite volatile. As noted earlier, the significance of changes in regulation is that they can change the transfer between claimants, exposing shareholders to greater residual risk than they expected and other stakeholders to residual risk where none was expected. From an SRI perspective, if environmental and social costs and benefits are not taken into account in the analysis of firm value, then it may be the case that cash flows assigned to equity in valuation models are too high or too low. Alternatively, it may be the case that the cost of equity is not correctly estimated, or indeed both.

The key point to note about the representation of the firm in Exhibit 6.4 is that the way to maximize the value of the firm is for management to maximize cash flows, shown on the right side of the exhibit. The cash flows then need to pass to the claimants in an equitable manner, as determined by the "nexus of contracts"

---

[71]For example, see Jensen (2003): "The corporation is the nexus for a complex set of voluntary contracts among customers, workers, managers, and the suppliers of materials, capital and risk bearing" (p. 1).

[72]See Fama and Jensen (1983b).

[73]See Fama and Jensen (1983a, p. 154).

©2006, The Research Foundation of CFA Institute

referred to previously. If any one of the claims becomes very large, it will compromise the others, which is where corporate governance is critical. Conceptualizing the firm as shown in Exhibit 6.4, of course, also suggests that different discount rates could be applied to each type of claim, affecting the relative proportions assigned to each claimant within the overall value of the firm.

Naturally, several practical problems are inherent in this approach. As noted in Chapter 4, it is likely to be impossible to separate out claims and cash flows as shown earlier. In addition, it is impossible to know whether the SRI issues perceived as relevant are reflected in share prices because the market cannot be observed.[74] This problem, however, is not specific to SRI. It is widely known to apply to any information identified as relevant in research.

The residual claims framework may well be the most promising with respect to an issue encountered in Chapters 2 and 3, namely, the difficulty of resolving conflicts between stakeholders. For adherents to the agency model, the objective is to maximize shareholder value; for adherents to the stakeholder approach, account must be taken of all relevant stakeholders. Jensen (2001) referred to an "enlightened stakeholder theory." The aim of his enlightened stakeholder approach is to maximize the value of the firm—that is, the total of the firm's equity, debt, and any other contingent claims.[75] The key point about Jensen's argument is perhaps that this approach gives company managers a means of making trade-offs between the many stakeholders in the firm. (In the preface, and in Chapter 3, this problem was framed as a conflict of interest problem.) As long as there is enough information in the public domain to permit the value of all relevant claims to be understood (see the importance of disclosure in Chapter 4), then the "enlightened stakeholder" approach may be the answer to many of the concerns raised by SRI practitioners. But as Chapter 4 also made clear, SRI practitioners spend a lot of time and energy working on disclosure. Information search costs remain relatively high for some of the claims.

Contingent Claims

As noted previously, the field of SRI is a source of new information (and regulation in related areas is often a source of event risk), and so a contingent claims approach is likely to be helpful to SRI specialists. A number of well-known models have been developed to value options. These models are more typically used in the context of options markets, but they can be applied to value claims on "real assets," so called

---

[74]See also the Roll (1977) critique of the CAPM.
[75]Conceptually speaking, it should then be possible for company management to consider an activity, such as mining, as the depletion of an asset that should, in some way, be made good. (Because such depletion is irreversible, this replenishing would have to be by adding value elsewhere or by reversing the decision to run the mine.)

to distinguish them from financial assets. The difference between a financial option and a real option is defined as follows by Howell, Stark, Newton, Paxson, Cavus, and Patel (2001):

> The key difference between a financial and a real option is that a decision about a financial option cannot change the value of the firm itself while a wrong decision about a real option will change the firm's resources and its value. For example, if a firm invests at the wrong time it will throw away part of the value of its "real option" to invest. (p. 7)

The EPA (1996), similarly, refers to the difference between actual and potential environmental liabilities. With respect to liabilities that are only potential, it is possible to modify business practices in order to avoid or reduce them. Similarly, potential assets of the future can be built up as a result of environmentally or socially driven innovation.

Real Options and SRI

Many potentially good examples of "real options" exist in the context of SRI. The earliest recognition of their potential was probably the 1871 work of Jevons in the area of environmental option value in the context of irreplaceable natural resources.[76] For example, an oil firm drilling for oil in a beauty spot has a choice: Go ahead without more ado, or negotiate access conditions with local stakeholders. Going ahead without negotiating may reduce up-front costs but is likely to result in substantial environmental costs. As a consequence, an important "social asset" of the firm may be wiped out: Access to other potential oil reserves may now be less than it was because competitors with a better environmental reputation may gain access right "share." The right to make future investment decisions, therefore, may be lost. Going ahead without negotiating could be seen as equivalent to throwing away a "real option." This approach could also be applied to "social" issues. For instance, in a human resources context, investment in training is likely to create real options—for instance, the flexibility to follow business opportunities requiring technical knowledge. But the extent to which such know-how can be obtained outside the firm (how easily replaceable it is) would also be relevant.

Exhibit 6.5 suggests how a real option framework might be applied in the context of a financial model, comparing the main features of environmental and social real options with real options as defined by Howell et al. (2001) and with equity itself framed as an "option" (or contingent claim) on the business.

---

[76]Cited in Paxson (1995).

Exhibit 6.5. Equity as an Option, Real Options, and SRI Real Options

Category	Equity	Real Option	Environmental/Social "Real Option"
Option	Market value of equity	Net present value of potential investment	Net present value of potential costs or benefits arising from an environmental or social liability or asset (residual claims)
Underlying	Market value of enterprise	Potential physical or other business assets	Potential environmental or social assets or liabilities
Exercise price	Market value of a firm's debt	Fixed price at which business investment can be made or sold	Price at which any potential environmental or social asset or liability may crystallize
Direction of rights	To buy or sell the shares	Opportunity to invest/ disinvest	Opportunity to invest/disinvest
Continuity	Continuous unless there is a market interruption	Variable	Variable

Source: Based on Howell et al. (2001, p. 19).

Putting the "real options" concept into the residual claims framework, Exhibit 6.4 can be amended, as shown in **Exhibit 6.6,** for firms having relevant contingent claims. In this case, the key point is that the way to maximize the value of the firm may be to avoid or minimize some contingent claims in order to avoid compromising the other claims (including the equity claim!) by taking out "insurance."

Exhibit 6.6. SRI Firm Value with Contingent Claims

Liabilities or "Claims" on the Business	Cash Flows
Equity	Dividends, other cash remaining to shareholders
Debt	Interest and principal and other relevant cash flows
Environmental and social (e.g., a known requirement to make good a depleted asset)	Cash flows generated by the environmental and social assets of the business (e.g., access to some raw materials having social value)
Contingent claims ("real options"—rights can be assigned to a specific stakeholder other than shareholder or lender). Potential environmental and social liabilities having some probability of crystallizing. Risk may be offset (see right).	Net present value of investment in, for example, pollution control. "Equivalent cash flow" arising from real options if "in the money." This is the value of a liability or cost avoided (see left).

Source: Adapted from Hudson (2005).

In Chapter 5, investment in environmental efficiency was seen to have production efficiency benefits. But it may enhance firm value in other ways—for instance, in the value of liabilities avoided.

Although this framework, conceptually speaking, holds potential for SRI, in practice, it is likely to be difficult to implement in view of the informational inputs needed.

Because markets are social as well as economic organizations, maximizing the total value of the organization's claims net of relevant costs and, of course, while maintaining a balance between claimants (stakeholders) through the firm's corporate governance practices is likely to be what makes the largest contribution to society as a whole (see also Jensen 2001). This chapter suggests (recalling Chapter 3) that it can be helpful to leverage off existing (and developing) theories of finance in order to connect the relevant social and environmental "claims" to finance when it is reasonable and feasible to do so.

©2006, The Research Foundation of CFA Institute

7. Summary and Conclusions

Socially responsible investment is sometimes thought to be synonymous with community investing and exclusion screening. Such approaches are perfectly valid in themselves if they meet the requirements of the relevant investor in the decision chain. But as this monograph should have made clear, SRI is a rather more complex discipline, bringing insights that can be relevant to anyone making investment decisions in a general sense. To assist the reader in digesting this complexity, the various approaches to SRI and the ways they relate to other disciplines and models widely used in finance have been summarized in a series of exhibits. For the four approaches to SRI (exclusion, best in class, engagement, and advocacy) identified in this work (and for some hybrid approaches), beliefs underlying the approach are summarized in Exhibit 1.2; the relevance of the prevalent corporate governance approach is found in Exhibit 2.3; likely beliefs about efficient markets, fund manager skill, and benchmarks are shown in Exhibit 5.1 and Exhibit 5.2; relevant tests of financial performance are discussed in Exhibit 5.3; and finally, SRI approaches and theoretical frameworks that appear to offer some rationale for the four approaches are contained in Exhibit 6.2.

Portfolio considerations must be the place to start for any asset manager considering an SRI investment approach because the return requirements, risk appetite, and constraints of the end investor in the portfolio (under the terms of the contract with the asset manager) should determine which approach is appropriate in the portfolio context. Equally important is the corporate governance climate within which firms in the portfolio are operating, which is likely to have an impact on the risk profile of stocks in the portfolio in different jurisdictions (see Exhibit 2.3).

SRI is an investment approach driven by the values of the investor. It is also driven by investor beliefs (see Exhibits 1.2 and 5.1) with respect to financial markets. The most important of these beliefs, in an investment context, may include the belief that the "invisible hand" does not always work to the greater good and that markets are not necessarily always efficient. The stance implied by an SRI investment approach with respect to market efficiency is consistent with welfare economics and the associated disciplines of development and regulation economics, which deal with market failure and, therefore, with inefficiency in a much broader sense. A consideration of SRI issues in the context of sector or company analysis may highlight situations in which firms may not be operating within (what the investor would see as) reasonable constraints, and if so, this information is likely to be a useful insight to investors assessing company risk profiles. In addition, it may highlight risk. Economic inefficiencies may involve an inefficient transfer of resources between stakeholders, and over time, this situation may reverse, whether because markets "correct" or because government bodies introduce new regulations or because consumers lobby to redress the balance.

When ownership and control are separated, as they are for most of the companies encountered in the context of portfolio investment, the issues highlighted by an SRI approach may at some stage affect those invested in residual claims, which is, of course, all equity investors and lenders in distressed situations. For residual claimants, the way a firm handles environmental, social, and ethical issues will be shaped by the firm's corporate governance practices; therefore, from the perspective of the investor as a stakeholder, the positioning of the firm with respect to all relevant stakeholders (and not the shareholder in isolation) is likely to provide an informative window into the firm's strategic direction and risk control. SRI investors working on the basis of an engagement approach are at times looking to influence the relationship between firms and their stakeholders with the aim of making sure that stakeholders (including shareholders) are fairly treated. In this regard, an approach referred to by Jensen (2001) as the "enlightened stakeholder theory" is likely to be relevant. The aim of this approach is to maximize the value of the entire firm.[77]

Markets are social organizations driven by human behavior and, particularly, crowd behavior. It is, therefore, conceivable that trends in exclusion investment may carry relevant information about paradigm shifts in society, and some of these paradigm shifts have indeed at times become relevant to financial markets. Best-in-class investors are, as a group, likely to influence the relationships between firms, markets, and society by setting up environmental and social criteria as a basis on which firms may have to compete for capital in financial markets and for success in their product markets. In short, best-in-class investors appear to be looking to leverage off market forces, implying a belief that markets can function effectively as an intermediary between the corporation and society. Similarly, engagement investors seek to influence firm behavior through the shareholder vote, and activist investors, by acting together. Whichever route is taken, any of these approaches can influence firms and markets and, therefore, may contain useful signaling information for all investors.

A key question to be addressed, with respect to firms, is what relevance CSR considerations have to the core business. Most financial analysts are familiar with the five forces of the Porter analysis. The social dimension of the Porter approach, and the relevance of the social dimension to finance, is (as observed in Chapter 3) often just a subtext in most analysis, and yet, the Porter framework can be said to encapsulate the dynamic between the major stakeholders in the corporation. As shown, Porter himself actively follows this line of research (Porter and Van der

---

[77]See also the French and Dutch corporate governance codes referred to in Chapter 2.

Linde 1995a and 1995b). The extent to which a firm incorporates (or not) environmental and social issues within its strategy, the structure of an industry as described by the Porter competitive framework, and a consideration of the potential flow of the cost benefits of economic activity between stakeholders (through a tool such as the "stakeholder balance sheet") may highlight opportunities and risks facing firms (see Chapter 3).

A key question for any person running investment portfolios with a duty to meet return benchmarks is whether the incorporation of SRI criteria into the investment decision-making process is unacceptable from a fiduciary standpoint. The key point here is likely to be the relevance of such information to the core business of firms in the portfolio (see Chapter 2 and also Chapter 4). The review of literature in Chapter 5 suggests that best-in-class operating performance may at times be associated with outperformance in asset markets. It also suggests that information in the "SRI" segment may be incorporated by markets with drift. If markets are effective as an intermediary between firms and society, there should be a two-way dynamic in operation—financial markets influencing firms and company performance (overall) having an impact on asset price performance.

For financial analysts, the main issues are obtaining sufficient information to apply "risk markers" to firms as a cohort (as described in Chapter 5) in order to be able to leverage off the theoretical models of finance, such as the Carhart (1997) model. Disclosure and reporting are evolving but still have some way to go before Black's (1980) dream of having sufficient information to derive consistent valuations through time and in cross-section can be attained. Financial models themselves are evolving. Who is to say what the leading-edge model will look like in another decade? The answer may depend on how reporting evolves. If information remains costly and disclosure does not evolve, one might expect social performance either to remain unexplained within usual models or to be a marker of management quality built into specialist predictive models. But if financial, social, and governance issues are sufficiently disclosed for research costs to fall sharply, then it is highly likely that they may become hidden somewhere within the model rather than being a separate "factor." Either way, improved disclosure should have the effect of making the apparent incorporation of such information with drift (see Derwall et al. 2005) disappear, which appears to be happening first for environmental performance. For other performance inputs highlighted by SRI approaches, it is still an open question.

In conclusion, SRI issues are of general relevance to any investor who does not subscribe to the concept of market (and economic) efficiency. Insofar as SRI is a stakeholder approach, it can act as an effective balance in situations in which the agency problem is present. Insofar as SRI aims at balance, there is also scope for it to work in the opposite direction should shareholders be so low in the pecking order that other stakeholders benefit disproportionately from economic activity and at the expense of shareholders.[78] Markets are, simply, social mechanisms. Just like any other social institution, they can be leveraged off for good or ill. At times, markets do a supremely good job of allocating resources properly, and at other times, they do not. The significance of this point to investors in the short run is that getting this right or wrong is likely to have financial consequences and, therefore, will affect portfolio investments. The broader significance is encapsulated by Schmookler (1993):

> The crucial element missing from traditional economic analysis is a long-term, social-evolutionary perspective. It may indeed be true that, in the static perspective that characterizes most economics, the market is almost right on the money, missing the ideal only slightly. But if one looks at the development of a society over time, even a small error—if it is systematic and constant—will lead to profound, potentially catastrophic distortion. (p. 25)

The discipline of SRI, therefore, has two important roles to play: (1) to recognize when it is reasonable and feasible to connect social and environmental issues to finance and (2) to recognize when they should not be so connected because market failure (see Chapter 2) is highly likely to follow any such attempt.

---

[78]Many shareholders invest in equities within their pension funds. If they are unfairly treated, this can also be a social issue!

  ©2006, The Research Foundation of CFA Institute

Appendix A. Principles

Ceres Principles

Protection of the biosphere:

We will reduce and make continual progress toward eliminating the release of any substance that may cause environmental damage to the air, water, or the earth or its inhabitants. We will safeguard all habitats affected by our operations and will protect open spaces and wilderness, while preserving biodiversity.

Sustainable use of natural resources:

We will make sustainable use of renewable natural resources, such as water, soils and forests. We will conserve non-renewable natural resources through efficient use and careful planning.

Reduction and disposal of wastes:

We will reduce and where possible eliminate waste through source reduction and recycling. All waste will be handled and disposed of through safe and responsible methods.

Energy conservation:

We will conserve energy and improve the energy efficiency of our internal operations and of the goods and services we sell. We will make every effort to use environmentally safe and sustainable energy sources.

Risk reduction:

We will strive to minimize the environmental, health and safety risks to our employees and the communities in which we operate through safe technologies, facilities and operating procedures, and by being prepared for emergencies.

Safe products and services:

We will reduce and where possible eliminate the use, manufacture or sale of products and services that cause environmental damage or health or safety hazards. We will inform our customers of the environmental impacts of our products or services and try to correct unsafe use.

Environmental Restoration:

We will promptly and responsibly correct conditions we have caused that endanger health, safety, or the environment. To the extent feasible, we will redress injuries we have caused to persons or damage we have caused to the environment and will restore the environment.

Informing the public:

We will inform in a timely manner everyone who may be affected by conditions caused by our company that might endanger health, safety or the environment. We will regularly seek advice and counsel through dialog with persons in communities near our facilities. We will not take any action against employees for reporting dangerous incidents or conditions to management or to appropriate authorities.

Management commitment:

We will implement these principles and sustain a process that ensures that the Board of Directors and Chief Executive Officer are fully informed about pertinent environmental issues and are fully responsible for environmental policy. In selecting our Board of Directors, we will consider demonstrated environmental commitment as a factor.

Audits and reports:

We will conduct an annual self-evaluation of our progress in implementing these principles. We will support the timely creation of generally accepted environmental audit procedures. We will annually complete the Ceres Report, which will be made available to the public.

Disclaimer: These principles establish an environmental ethic with criteria by which investors and others can assess the environmental performance of companies. Companies that endorse these principles pledge to go voluntarily beyond the requirements of the law. The terms "may" and "might" in Principles one and eight are not meant to encompass every imaginable consequence, no matter how remote. Rather, these principles obligate endorsers to behave as prudent persons who are not governed by conflicting interests and who possess a strong commitment to environmental excellence and to human health and safety. These principles are not intended to create new legal liabilities, expand existing rights or obligations, waive legal defenses, or otherwise affect the legal position of any endorsing company, and are not intended to be used against an endorser in any legal proceeding for any purpose.

Source: Ceres.

Global Sullivan Principles

Express our support for universal human rights and, particularly, those of our employees, the communities within which we operate, and partners with whom we do business.

Promote equal opportunity for our employees at all levels of the company with respect to issues such as color, race, gender, age, ethnicity, religious beliefs, and operate without unacceptable worker treatment such as the exploitation of children, physical punishment, female abuse, involuntary servitude, or other forms of abuse.

Respect our employees' voluntary freedom of association.

Compensate our employees to enable them to meet at least their basic needs and provide the opportunity to improve their skill and capability in order to raise their social and economic opportunities.

Provide a safe and healthy workplace; protect human health and the environment; and promote sustainable development.

Promote fair competition including respect for intellectual and other property rights, and not offer, pay, or accept bribes.

Work with governments and communities in which we do business to improve the quality of life in those communities—their educational, cultural, economic, and social well-being—and seek to provide training and opportunities for workers from disadvantaged backgrounds.

Promote the application of these principles by those with whom we business.

Source: The Leon H. Sullivan Foundation.

UN Global Compact: The Ten Principles

Area/Principle

Human rights

Principle 1: Business should support and respect the protection of internationally proclaimed human rights, and

Principle 2: make sure that they are not complicit in human rights abuses.

Labor standards

Principle 3: Businesses should uphold the freedom of association and the effective recognition of the right to collective bargaining;

Principle 4: the elimination of all forms of forced and compulsory labor;

Principle 5: the effective abolition of child labor; and

Principle 6: the elimination of discrimination in respect of employment and occupation.

Environment

Principle 7: Businesses should support a precautionary approach to environmental challenges;

Principle 8: undertake initiatives to promote greater environmental responsibility; and

Principle 9: encourage the development and diffusion of environmentally friendly technologies.

Anticorruption

Principle 10: Businesses should work against all forms of corruption, including extortion and bribery.

Notes: See also the Universal Declaration of Human Rights, the International Labor Organization's Declaration on Fundamental Principles and Rights at Work, the Rio Declaration on Environment and Development, and the UN Convention Against Corruption. The Ten Principles are derived from these declarations.

Source: The UN Global Compact.

Appendix B. List of Websites

AccountAbility	www.accountability.org.uk
Association of British Insurers	www.abi.org.uk
Calvert Group	www.calvertgroup.com
Ceres	www.ceres.org
Citizens Funds	www.efund.com
Core Ratings/DNV	www.dnv.com
Deminor	www.deminor.org
Dow Jones Sustainability Indexes	www.sustainability-indexes.com
Enhanced Analytics Initiative (EAI)	www.enhancedanalytics.com
ENERGY STAR program	www.energystar.gov
ENERGY STAR program (Japan), through Energy Conservation Center	www.eccj.or.jp
The Equator Principles	www.equator-principles.com
Ethical Investment Research Services (EIRIS)	www.eiris.org
European Corporate Governance Service (ECGS)	www.ecgs.net
European Union	http://europa.eu.int
FTSE	www.ftse.com
GES Investment Services	www.ges-invest.com
Global Reporting Initiative (GRI)	www.globalreporting.org
Global Sullivan Principles of Social Responsibility	www.thesullivanfoundation.org/gsp
Good Bankers Co.	www.goodbankers.co.jp
GovernanceMetrics International (GMI)	www.gmiratings.com
Innovest Strategic Value Advisors	www.innovestgroup.com
Institute for Strategy and Competitiveness (see Michael E. Porter publications)	www.isc.hbs.edu
Institutional Shareholder Services (ISS)	www.issproxy.com
Interfaith Center on Corporate Responsibility (ICCR)	www.iccr.org
International Accounting Standards Board	www.iasb.co.uk
International Organization for Standardization (ISO)	www.iso.org
Investor Responsibility Research Center (IRRC)	www.irrc.org
KLD Research & Analytics	www.kld.com
Organisation for Economic Co-Operation and Development (OECD)	www.oecd.org
RWE Group	www.rwe.com

SIRAN (Social Investment Research Analyst Network)	www.siran.org
SiRi Company	www.siricompany.com
Social Investment Forum	
UKSIF	www.uksif.org
SIF (U.S.)	www.socialinvest.org
Eurosif	www.eurosif.org
SocialFunds.com	www.socialfunds.com
Sullivan Foundation (Leon H.)	www.thesullivanfoundation.org
Trucost	www.trucost.com
United Nations Global Compact	www.unglobalcompact.org
UNEP Finance Initiative	www.unepfi.org
Vigeo	www.vigeo.com
World Economic Forum	www.weforum.org
World Resources Institute	www.wri.org

©2006, The Research Foundation of CFA Institute

References

ABI. 2001. "Investing in Social Responsibility: Risks and Opportunities." ABI Research Reports. London, U.K.: Association of British Insurers.

———. 2002. *Guidance on Corporate Social Responsibility Management and Reporting for the Financial Services Sector: A Practical Toolkit.* London, U.K.: Association of British Insurers (1 November).

AccountAbility. 1999. AccountAbility 1000 Framework.

Admati, Anat R., Paul Pfleiderer, and Josef Zechner. 1994. "Large Shareholder Activism, Risk Sharing, and Financial Market Equilibrium." *Journal of Political Economy,* vol. 102, no. 6 (December):1097–1130.

ASB. 2005. Reporting Standard (RS) 1: *The Operating and Financial Review.* Accounting Standards Board (May).

Austin, Duncan, and Amanda Sauer. 2002. "Changing Oil: Emerging Environmental Risks and Shareholder Value in the Oil and Gas Industry." Research report, World Resources Institute.

Austin, Duncan, Niki Rosinski, Amanda Sauer, and Colin Le Duc. 2003. "Changing Drivers: The Impact of Climate Change on Competitiveness and Value Creation in the Automotive Industry." Research report, World Resources Institute and Sustainable Asset Management (SAM).

Bakan, Joel. 2004. *The Corporation: The Pathological Pursuit of Profit and Power.* London, U.K.: Constable.

Banz, Rolf W. 1981. "The Relationship between Return and Market Value of Common Stocks." *Journal of Financial Economics*, vol. 9, no. 1 (March):3–18.

Bauer, R., K. Koedijk, and R. Otten. 2002. "International Evidence on Ethical Mutual Fund Performance and Investment Style." Working paper, Limburg Institute of Financial Economics (November).

Bauer, Rob, Roger Otten, and Alireza Tourani Rad. 2004. "Ethical Investing in Australia: Is There a Financial Penalty?" Working paper, Limburg Institute of Financial Economics (January).

Bennett, Martin, Pall M. Rikhardsson, and Stefan Schaltegger, *eds.* 2003. *Environmental Management Accounting: Purpose and Progress.* Dordrecht, Netherlands: Kluwer Academic Publishers.

Berle, Adolf A., and Gardiner C. Means. 2003. *The Modern Corporation and Private Property.* Reprinted, with a new introduction by Mark Jensen and Murray L. Weidenbaum. Somerset, NJ: Transaction Publishers. (Originally published in 1932.)

Black, Fischer. 1980. "The Magic in Earnings: Economic Earnings versus Accounting Earnings." *Financial Analysts Journal*, vol. 36, no. 6 (November/December):19–42.

Boardman, Anthony E., David H. Greenberg, Aidan R. Vining, and David L. Weimer. 2001. *Cost-Benefit Analysis: Concepts and Practice.* 2nd ed. Upper Saddle River, NJ: Prentice Hall.

Cadbury, Adrian. 2002. *Corporate Governance and Chairmanship: A Personal View.* Oxford, U.K.: Oxford University Press.

Cadbury Committee. 1992. "The Financial Aspects of Corporate Governance." Cadbury Report (December).

Cahan, Steven F. 1992. "The Effect of Antitrust Investigations on Discretionary Accruals: A Refined Test of the Political Cost Hypothesis." *Accounting Review*, vol. 67, no. 1 (January):77–95.

Carhart, Mark M. 1997. "On Persistence in Mutual Fund Performance." *Journal of Finance*, vol. 52, no. 1 (March):57–82.

Cheffins, Brian R. 2002. "Putting Britain on the ROE Map: The Emergence of the Berle–Means Corporation in the United Kingdom." In *Corporate Governance Regimes: Convergence and Diversity.* Edited by Joseph A. McCahery, Piet Moerland, Theo Raaijmakers, and Luc Renneboog. Oxford, U.K.: Oxford University Press.

Cohen, Mark A., Scott A. Fenn, and Shameek Konar. 1997. "Environmental and Financial Performance: Are They Related?" Working paper, Vanderbilt University.

Commission of the German Corporate Governance Code. 2005. "German Corporate Governance Code." Dusseldorf, Germany: (amended 2 June): www.corporate-governance-code.de/eng/download/E_CorGov_Endfassung2005.pdf.

Corbett, Charles J., and Robert D. Klassen. 2006. "Extending the Horizons: Environmental Excellence as Key to Improving Operations." *Manufacturing & Service Operations Management*, vol. 8, no. 1 (Winter):5–22.

Conference Board Commission on Public Trust and Private Enterprise. 2003. *Part 2, Corporate Governance: Principles, Recommendations and Specific Best Practice Suggestions*. New York: The Conference Board (9 January).

Dasgupta, Susmita, Benoit Laplante, and Nlandu Mamingi. 1997. "Capital Market Responses to Environmental Performance in Developing Countries." Working Paper 1909, World Bank Development Research Group (October).

Dechow, Patricia M., and Catherine M. Schrand. 2004. *Earnings Quality*. Charlottesville, VA: Research Foundation of CFA Institute.

Dechow, Patricia M., Richard G. Sloan, and Amy P. Sweeney. 1996. "Causes and Consequences of Earnings Manipulation: An Analysis of Firms Subject to Enforcement Actions by the SEC." *Contemporary Accounting Research*, vol. 13, no. 1 (Spring):1–36.

DEFRA. 2001. *General Guidelines on Environmental Reporting*. London, U.K.: Department for Environment, Food and Rural Affairs.

De Jong, Abe, Rezaul Kabir, Teye Marra, and Ailsa Röell. 2001. "Ownership and Controls in the Netherlands." Chapter 7 in *The Control of Corporate Europe*. Edited by Fabrizio Barca and Marco Becht. Oxford, U.K.: Oxford University Press.

Derwall, Jeroen, Nadja Guenster, Rob Bauer, and Kees Koedijk. 2005. "The Eco-Efficiency Premium Puzzle." *Financial Analysts Journal*, vol. 61, no. 2 (March/April):51–63.

Diltz, J. David. 1995. "Does Social Screening Affect Portfolio Performance?" *Journal of Investing*, vol. 4, no. 1 (Spring):64–69.

Donaldson, Lex, and James H. Davis. 1991. "Stewardship Theory or Agency Theory: CEO Governance and Shareholder Returns." *Australian Journal of Management*, vol. 16, no. 1 (June):49–64.

Dowell, Glen, Stuart Hart, and Bernard Yeung. 2000. "Do Corporate Global Environmental Standards Create or Destroy Market Value?" *Management Science*, vol. 46, no. 8 (August):1059–1074.

Dutch Corporate Governance Code. 2003. The Hague, Netherlands: Corporate Governance Committee (http://corpgov.nl/page/downloads/CODE%20DEF%20ENGELS%20COMPLEET%20III.pdf).

Ehrbar, Al. 1998. *EVA: The Real Key to Creating Wealth*. New York: John Wiley & Sons, Inc.

Elkington, John. 1999. *Cannibals with Forks: The Triple Bottom Line of 21st Century Business*. Oxford, U.K.: Capstone Publishing.

EPA. 1996. "Valuing Potential Environmental Liabilities for Managerial Decision-Making: A Review of Available Techniques." U.S. Environmental Protection Agency 742-R-96-003 (December).

———. 2003. "Identifying and Calculating Economic Benefit That Goes Beyond Avoided and/or Delayed Costs." U.S. Environmental Protection Agency, Office of Enforcement and Compliance Monitoring (May).

Esty, Daniel C., and Michael E. Porter. 1998. "Industrial Ecology and Competitiveness: Strategic Implications for the Firm." *Journal of Industrial Ecology*, vol. 2, no. 1 (Winter):35–44.

European Commission. 2001. "Commission Recommendation of 30 May 2001 on the Recognition, Measurement and Disclosure of Environmental Issues in the Annual Accounts and Annual Reports of Companies" (2001/453/EC). *Official Journal of the European Communities*, L 156 (13 June):33–42 (www.iasplus.com/resource/0105euroenv.pdf).

European Union. 1996. *Integrated Pollution Prevention and Control (IPPC) Directive* (96/16/EC): http://ec.europa.eu/environment/air/legis.htm#stationary.

Eurosif. 2003. "Socially Responsible Investment among European Institutional Investors." Research report, Eurosif.

F&C Asset Management and UBS. 2005. *HIV/AIDS Beyond Africa: Managing the Financial Impacts* (12 May).

Fama, Eugene F., and Kenneth R. French. 1993. "Common Risk Factors in the Returns on Bonds and Stocks." *Journal of Financial Economics*, vol. 33, no. 1 (February):3–56.

Fama, Eugene F., and Michael C. Jensen. 1983a. "Agency Problems and Residual Claims." *Journal of Law and Economics*, vol. 26, no. 2 (June):327–349. Reprinted in Michael C. Jensen, *Foundations of Organizational Strategy* (Cambridge, MA: Harvard University Press, 1998).

———. 1983b. "Separation of Ownership and Control." *Journal of Law and Economics*, vol. 26, no. 2 (June):301–325. Reprinted in Michael C. Jensen, *Foundations of Organizational Strategy* (Cambridge, MA: Harvard University Press, 1998).

Feldman, S., P. Soyka, and P. Ameer. 1997. "Does Improving a Firm's Environmental Management System and Environmental Performance Result in a Higher Stock Price?" *Journal of Investing*, vol. 6, no. 4 (Winter):87–97.

Filbeck, Greg, and Raymond F. Gorman. 2004. "The Stock Price Reaction to Environmentally-Related Company News." *Journal of Business and Public Affairs*, vol. 31, no. 1 (Fall):25–31.

FORGE Group. 2002. *Guidelines on Environmental Management and Reporting for the Financial Services Sector: A Practical Toolkit*. London, U.K.: Association of British Insurers (www.abi.org.uk/forge/ForgeText.htm).

Franks, Julian, and Colin Mayer. 1997. "Corporate Ownership and Control in the U.K., Germany, and France." Chapter 23 in *Studies in International Corporate Finance and Governance Systems: A Comparison of the U.S., Japan, and Europe*. Edited by Donald H. Chew. Oxford, U.K.: Oxford University Press.

Frederick, Shane, George Loewenstein, and Ted O'Donoghue. 2002. "Time Discounting and Time Preference: A Critical Review." *Journal of Economic Literature*, vol. 40 (June):351–401.

Freshfields Bruckhaus Deringer. 2005. "A Legal Framework for the Integration of Environmental, Social and Governance Issues into Institutional Investment." UNEP Financial Initiative (www.unepfi.org/fileadmin/documents/freshfields_legal_resp_20051123.pdf).

Friedman, Milton. 1970. "The Social Responsibility of Business Is to Increase Its Profits." *New York Times Magazine* (13 September):32–33.

FSA. 2003. "Combined Code on Corporate Governance." London, U.K.: Financial Services Authority (July): www.fsa.gov.uk/pubs/ukla/lr_comcode2003.pdf.

Garber, S., and J.K. Hammitt. 1998. "Risk Premiums for Environmental Liability: Does Superfund Increase the Cost of Capital?" *Journal of Environmental Economics and Management*, vol. 36, no. 3 (November):267–294.

Geczy, Christopher C., Robert F. Stambaugh, and David Levin. 2003. "Investing in Socially Responsible Mutual Funds." Working paper (May).

Girard, Eric, Brett Stone, and Hamid Rahman. 2005. "Socially Responsible Investments: Goody-Two-Shoes or Bad to the Bone?" Working paper, Siena College, Loudonville, NY, and Alliant International University, San Diego, CA.

Gompers, Paul A., Joy L. Ishii, and Andrew Metrick. 2001. "Corporate Governance and Equity Prices." National Bureau of Economic Research Working Paper 8449.

Govindaraj, Suresh, Bikki Jaggi, and Beixin Lin. 2004. "Market Overreaction to Product Recall Revisited—The Case of Firestone Tires and the Ford Explorer." *Review of Quantitative Finance and Accounting*, vol. 23, no. 1 (July):31–54.

Gregory, A., J. Matatko, and R. Luther. 1997. "Ethical Unit Trust Financial Performance: Small Company Effects and Fund Size Effects." *Journal of Business Finance & Accounting*, vol. 24, no. 5:705–725.

Grossman, Sanford J., and Joseph E. Stiglitz. 1980. "On the Impossibility of Informationally Efficient Markets." *American Economic Review*, vol. 70, no. 3 (June):393–408.

Guenster, Nadja, Jeroen Derwall, and Rob Bauer. 2005. "The Economic Value of Corporate Eco-Efficiency." Working Paper 05-09, Limburg Institute of Financial Economics.

Guerard, J.B. 1997. "Is There a Cost to Being Socially Responsible in Investing?" *Journal of Investing*, vol. 6, no. 2 (Summer):11–18.

Hamilton, J. 1995. "Pollution as News: Media and Stock Market Reactions to the Toxics Release Inventory Data." *Journal of Environmental Economics and Management*, vol. 28, no. 1 (January):98–113.

Hamilton, Kirk, and Ernst Lutz. 1996. *Green National Accounts: Policy Uses and Empirical Experience.* Environment Department Paper Number 39. Washington, DC: World Bank, Environment Department, Vice Presidency for Environmentally Sustainable Development.

Hampel Committee (Committee on Corporate Governance). 1998. "Final Report." U.K. Committee on Corporate Governance (January).

Hart, Stuart L., and Gautam Ahuja. 1996. "Does It Pay to Be Green? An Empirical Examination of the Relationship between Emission Reduction and Firm Performance." *Business Strategy and the Environment*, vol. 5, no. 1 (March):30–37.

Healey, Paul, and Robert S. Kaplan. 1985. "The Effect of Bonus Schemes on Accounting Decisions." *Journal of Accounting and Economics*, vol. 7, nos. 1–3 (April):85–112.

Hemley, David, Donald Morris, and Christian Gilde. 2005. "Antisocially Conscious Sectors: A Benchmark for Socially Conscious Investing." *Journal of Investing*, vol. 14, no. 3 (Fall):78–82.

Henriques, Adrian, and Julie Richardson, *eds.* 2004. *The Triple Bottom Line: Does It All Add Up? Assessing the Sustainability of Business and CSR.* London, U.K.: Earthscan.

Howell, Sydney, Andrew Stark, David Newton, Dean Paxson, Mustafa Cavus, and Kanak Patel. 2001. *Real Options: Evaluating Corporate Investment Opportunities in a Dynamic World*. London, U.K: Financial Times Management.

Hudson, Julie. 2005. "Why Try to Quantify the Unquantifiable?" Research report, UBS Investment Research (April).

Hussein, Khaled, and Mohammed Omran. 2005. "Ethical Investment Revisited: Evidence from Dow Jones Islamic Indexes." *Journal of Investing*, vol. 14, no. 3 (Fall):105–126.

IASB. 2004. *International Financial Reporting Standards (IFRS)*. London, U.K.: International Accounting Standards Board.

Innovest Strategic Value Advisors. 2005. "Carbon Disclosure Project 2005." Research report, Innovest Strategic Value Advisors (February).

Jensen, Michael C. 2001. "Value Maximization, Stakeholder Theory, and the Corporate Objective Function." *Journal of Applied Corporate Finance*, vol. 14, no. 3 (Fall):8–21.

———. 2003. *A Theory of the Firm: Governance, Residual Claims, and Organizational Forms*. Cambridge, MA: Harvard University Press.

Jones, Thomas M. 1995. "Instrumental Stakeholder Theory: A Synthesis of Ethics and Economics." *Academy of Management Review*, vol. 20, no. 2 (April):404–437.

Keown, A., and J. Pinkerton. 1981. "Merger Announcements and Insider Trading Activity: An Empirical Investigation." *Journal of Finance*, vol. 36, no. 3 (June):855–869.

Khanna, Madhu, and Surender Kumar. 2005. "Corporate Environmental Management and Environmental Efficiency." Working paper (September).

Khanna, Madhu, Surender Kumar, and Wilma Rose Q. Anton. 2004. "Environmental Self-Regulation: Implications for Environmental Efficiency and Profitability." Working paper (October).

Kinder, Peter D. 2005. "New Fiduciary Duties in a Changing Social Environment." *Journal of Investing*, vol. 14, no. 3 (Fall):24–40.

King, Andrew A., and Michael J. Lenox. 2001. "Does It *Really* Pay to Be Green? An Empirical Study of Firm Environmental and Financial Performance." *Journal of Industrial Ecology*, vol. 5, no. 1 (March):105–116.

Klassen, Robert D., and Curtis P. McLaughlin. 1996. "The Impact of Environmental Management on Firm Performance." *Management Science*, vol. 42, no. 8 (August):1199–1214.

Konar, Shameek, and Mark A. Cohen. 1997. "Information as Regulation: The Effect of Community Right to Know Laws on Toxic Emissions." *Journal of Environmental Economics and Management*, vol. 32, no. 1 (January):109–124.

———. 2000. "Why Do Firms Pollute (and Reduce) Toxic Emissions?" Working paper, Owen Graduate School of Management, Vanderbilt University.

———. 2001. "Does the Market Value Environmental Performance?" *Review of Economics and Statistics*, vol. 8, no. 2 (May):281–289.

KPMG. 2005. *International Survey of Corporate Responsibility Reporting 2005*. Amsterdam, Netherlands: KPMG International.

Kreander, N., R.H. Gray, D.M. Power, and C.D. Sinclair. 2005. "Evaluating the Performance of Ethical and Non-Ethical Funds: A Matched Pair Analysis." *Journal of Business Finance & Accounting*, vol. 32, nos. 7–8 (September):1465–1493.

Kurtz, Lloyd, and Dan diBartolomeo. 2005. "The KLD Catholic Values 400 Index." *Journal of Investing*, vol. 14, no. 3 (Fall):101–104.

Lichfield, Nathaniel, Peter Kettle, and Michael Whitbread. 1975. *Evaluation in the Planning Process*. Oxford, U.K.: Pergamon Press.

Lindenberg, E.B., and Stephen A. Ross. 1981. "Tobin's *q* Ratio and Industrial Organization." *Journal of Business*, vol. 54, no. 1 (January):1–32.

Lyndenberg, Steven. 2005. "Social and Environmental Data as New Tools." *Journal of Investing*, vol. 14, no. 3 (Fall):40–47.

Mahoney, Lois, and Robin W. Roberts. 2002. "Corporate Social and Environmental Performance and Their Relation to Financial Performance and Institutional Ownership: Empirical Evidence on Canadian Firms." Paper presented at the AAA Annual Meeting, San Antonio, Texas (August).

Margolis, Joshua Daniel, and James Patrick Walsh. 2001. *People and Profits? The Search for a Link between a Company's Social and Financial Performance*. Mahwah, NJ: Lawrence Erlbaum Associates.

Marklund, Per-Olov. 2003. "Environmental Regulation and Firm Efficiency: Studying the Porter Hypothesis Using a Directional Output Distance Function." Umeå Economic Studies Working Paper 619, Umeå University (December).

Martin, Stephen. 1993. *Advanced Industrial Economics*. Cambridge, MA: Blackwell.

Mas-Colell, Andreu, Michael D. Whinston, and Jerry R. Green. 1995. *Microeconomic Theory*. New York: Oxford University Press.

Mason, Edward. 1958. "The Apologetics of Managerialism." *Journal of Business*, vol. 31, no. 1:1–11.

McCahery, Joseph A., Piet Moerland, Theo Raajimakers, and Luc Renneboog, *eds*. 2002. *Corporate Governance Regimes: Convergence and Diversity*. Oxford, U.K.: Oxford University Press.

McDaniel, Jeff S., Vinay V. Gadkari, and Joseph Fiksel. 2000. "The Environmental EVA: A Financial Indicator for EH&S Strategists." *Corporate Environmental Strategy*, vol. 7, no. 2:125–136.

Milevsky, Moshe, Andrew Aziz, Al Goss, Jane Thomson, and David Wheeler. 2004. "Cleaning a Passive Index: How to Use Portfolio Optimization to Satisfy CSR Constraints." Working paper (December).

Moerland, P.W. 2002. "Complete Separation of Ownership and Control: The Structure-Regime and Other Defensive Mechanisms in the Netherlands." Chapter 12 in *Corporate Governance Regimes: Convergence and Diversity*. Edited by Joseph A. McCahery, Piet Moerland, Theo Raajimakers, and Luc Renneboog. Oxford, U.K.: Oxford University Press.

Monks, Robert A.G., and Nell Minow. 2001. *Corporate Governance*. 2nd ed. Cambridge, MA: Blackwell Business. (Originally published in 1995.)

Murphy, Christopher J. 2002. "The Profitable Correlation between Environmental and Financial Performance: A Review of the Research." Research report, Light Green Advisors.

Navarro, Peter. 1988. "Why Do Corporations Give to Charity?" *Journal of Business*, vol. 61, no. 1 (January):65–93.

Nehrt, Chad. 1996. "Timing and Intensity Effects of Environmental Investments." *Strategic Management Journal*, vol. 17, no. 7 (July):535–547.

OECD. 2000. "Guidelines for Multinational Enterprises: Revision 2000." London, U.K.: Organisation for Economic Co-Operation and Development (June): www.oecd.org/dataoecd/56/36/1922428.pdf.

Ozawa, Terutomo. 2000. "Japanese Firms in Deepening Integration: Evolving Corporate Governance." Chapter 12 in *Corporate Governance and Globalization: Long Range Planning Issues*. Edited by Stephen S. Cohen and Gavin Boyd. Cheltenham, U.K.: Edward Elgar.

Patten, Dennis M., and Greg Trompeter. 2003. "Corporate Responses to Political Costs: An Examination of the Relation between Environmental Disclosure and Earnings Management." *Journal of Accounting and Public Policy*, vol. 22, no. 1 (January–February):83–94.

Pava, Moses L., and Joshua Krausz. 1996. "The Association between Corporate Social-Responsibility and Financial Performance: The Paradox of Social Cost." *Journal of Business Ethics*, vol. 15, no. 3 (March):321–357.

Paxson, Dean A. 1995. "The Option Value in Environmental Economics." Working paper, Manchester Business School (January).

Peters Committee (Committee on Corporate Governance). 1997. "Corporate Governance in the Netherlands: Forty Recommendations." Committee on Corporate Governance, The Netherlands (June).

Porter, Michael E. 1992. *Capital Choices: Changing the Way America Invests in Industry*. Washington, DC: Council on Competitiveness and Harvard Business School.

———. 1998. *The Competitive Advantage of Nations*. New York: Free Press.

Porter, Michael E., and Claas van der Linde. 1995a. "Green and Competitive: Ending the Stalemate." *Harvard Business Review*, vol. 73, no. 5b (September/October):120–134.

———. 1995b. "Toward a New Conception of the Environment-Competitiveness Relationship." *Journal of Economic Perspectives*, vol. 9, no. 4 (Fall):97–118.

Reinganum, Marc R. 1981. "Misspecification of Capital Asset Pricing: Empirical Anomalies Based on Earnings Yields and Market Values." *Journal of Financial Economics*, vol. 9, no. 1 (March):19–46.

Repetto, Robert, and Duncan Austin. 2000. "Pure Profit: The Financial Implications of Environmental Performance." Research report, World Resources Institute (http://pubs.wri.org/pureprofit-pub-3026.html).

Roberts, Clare, Pauline Weetman, and Paul Gordon. 1998. *International Financial Accounting: A Comparative Approach*. London, U.K.: Financial Times/Pitman Publishing.

 ©2006, The Research Foundation of CFA Institute

Rockness, J.W., P. Schlachter, and H. Rockness. 1986. "Hazardous Waste Disposal, Corporate Disclosure, and Financial Performance in the Chemical Industry." In *Advances in Public Interest Accounting, Volume 1*. Edited by M. Neimark. Greenwich, CT: JAI Press.

Roe, Mark J. 1994. *Strong Managers, Weak Owners: The Political Roots of American Corporate Finance*. Princeton, NJ: Princeton University Press.

Roll, Richard. 1977. "A Critique of the Asset Pricing Theory's Tests, Part I: On Past and Potential Testability of the Theory." *Journal of Financial Economics*, vol. 4, no. 2 (March):129–176.

Romano, Roberta. 2002. "Less Is More: Making Institutional Investor Activism a Valuable Mechanism of Corporate Governance." Chapter 23 in *Corporate Governance Regimes: Convergence and Diversity*. Edited by Joseph A. McCahery, Piet Moerland, Theo Raajimakers, and Luc Renneboog. Oxford, U.K.: Oxford University Press.

Russo, Michael V., and Paul A. Fouts. 1997. "A Resource-Based Perspective on Corporate Environmental Performance and Profitability." *Academy of Management Journal. Academy of Management*, vol. 40, no. 3:534–559.

Sakuma, Kyoko. 2001. "Chapter 12: Japan." In *Corporate Governance and Economic Performance*. Edited by Klaus Gugler. Oxford, U.K.: Oxford University Press.

Sauer, Amanda, Philipp Mettler, Fred Wellington, and Gabriela Grab Hartmann. 2005. "Transparency Issues with the ACEA Agreement: Are Investors Driving Blindly?" Research report, World Resources Institute (March).

Sauer, David A. 1997. "The Impact of Social-Responsibility Screens on Investment Performance: Evidence from the Domini 400 Social Index and Domini Equity Mutual Fund." *Review of Financial Economics*, vol. 6, no. 2:137–149.

Shleifer, Andrei. 2000. *Inefficient Markets: An Introduction to Behavioral Finance*. Oxford, U.K.: Oxford University Press.

Shleifer, Andrei, and Robert W. Vishny. 1986. "Large Shareholders and Corporate Control." *Journal of Political Economy*, vol. 94, no. 3:461–488.

Schmookler, Andrew Bard. 1993. *The Illusion of Choice: How the Market Economy Shapes Our Destiny*. Albany, NY: State University of New York Press.

Smart, Bruce. 1992. *Beyond Compliance: A New Industry View of the Environment*. Washington, DC: World Resources Institute.

Smith, Tim. 2005. "Institutional and Social Investors Find Common Ground." *Journal of Investing*, vol. 14, no. 3 (Fall):57–66.

Social Investment Forum. 2003. "2003 Report on Socially Responsible Investing Trends in the United States." SIF Industry Research Program (December).

Sparkes, Russell. 2002. *Socially Responsible Investment: A Global Revolution.* New York: John Wiley & Sons.

Stapleton, Geof P., and Jonathan J. Bates. 2002. "Reducing the Costs of Proxy Voting." Chapter 24 in *Corporate Governance Regimes: Convergence and Diversity.* Edited by Joseph A. McCahery, Piet Moerland, Theo Raajimakers, and Luc Renneboog. Oxford, U.K.: Oxford University Press.

Statman, Meir. 2000. "Socially Responsible Mutual Funds." *Financial Analysts Journal*, vol. 56, no. 3 (May/June):30–39.

————. 2005a. "The Religions of Social Responsibility." *Journal of Investing*, vol. 14, no. 3 (Fall):14–21.

————. 2005b. "Socially Responsible Indexes: Composition and Performance." Working paper, Leavey School of Business, Santa Clara University (January).

Stone, Bernell K., John B. Guerard, Jr., Mustafa L. Gultekin, and Greg Adams. 2001. "Socially Responsible Investment Screening: Strong Evidence of No Significant Cost for Actively Managed Portfolios." Working paper.

Troutman, Michael. 2001. "Risk Control Techniques for Social Investing." *Journal of Investing*, vol. 10, no. 4 (Winter):51–57.

Trucost. 2004. "Environmental Disclosures." Research report, Environment Agency (U.K.): www.trucost.com/FTSEdisclosure.html.

UN Division for Sustainable Development. 2001. "Environmental Management Accounting Procedures and Principles." New York: UN (www.emawebsite.org/documents/emaric_139.pdf).

UN, EC, IMF, OECD, and World Bank. 2003. *Handbook of National Accounting: Integrated Environmental and Economic Accounting.* UN, European Commission, International Monetary Fund, OECD (http://unstats.un.org/unsd/envAccounting/seea2003.pdf).

UN Global Compact. 2004. "Who Cares Wins: Connecting Financial Markets to a Changing World." Research report, UN and Swiss Federal Department of Foreign Affairs (www.unglobalcompact.org/docs/news_events/8.1/WhoCaresWins.pdf).

Vermeir, Wim, Eveline Van De Velde, and Filip Corten. 2005. "Sustainable and Responsible Performance." *Journal of Investing*, vol. 14, no. 3 (Fall):94–101.

Viénot Report. 1995. "Le Conseil d'Administration des Sociétés Cotees, Rapport du Groupe de Travail." Association Française des Entreprises Privées, Conseil National du Patronat Français (July).

Waddock, Sandra A., and Samuel B. Graves. 1997. "The Corporate Social Performance-Financial Performance Link." *Strategic Management Journal*, vol. 18, no. 4 (April):303–319.

Weitzman, Martin. 1994. "On the Environmental Discount Rate." *Journal of Environmental Economics and Management*, vol. 26, no. 2:200–209.

White, Mark A. 1996. "Investor Response to the Exxon Valdez Oil Spill." Working paper, McIntire School of Commerce, University of Virginia.

World Economic Forum. 2005. "Statement of G8 Climate Change Round Table." Geneva: World Economic Forum (9 June): www.weforum.org/pdf/ g8_climatechange.pdf.